CW01594683

Islamic Studies Textbook Level 5

Series Editors

Waqas Ahmed Amin

Jawed Iqbal Tahiri

Mariam Khalid

Series Director

Tahseen Khalid

Minhaj-ul-Quran International

Preface

In the name of Allah, the Most Merciful, the Most Kind.

WE PRAISE ALLAH that the Muslim community has come a long way since the days when the first immigrants settled in Britain. From that time till today, there have been significant developments in the quality of educational material being produced by British Muslims. Many advancements have been made in this regard such that English is fast becoming one of the academic languages of Islam, alongside Arabic, Persian, Urdu and Turkish.

The importance of education cannot be overstated. The British Muslim community has put great effort into imparting Islamic knowledge to their children. Islamic classes and religious seminaries have been established up and down the country for the single goal of teaching the coming generations the fundamentals of their religion. Among those that have been at the forefront in this regard is Minhaj-ul-Quran International, a global organisation with branches in over 90 countries.

As an organisation, Minhaj-ul-Quran International seeks to uplift Muslims worldwide through the revival of education and spirituality. It established its first branch in the United Kingdom in the late 1980s and founded its first centre in the 1990s. For more than two decades it has endeavoured to provide for the educational and spiritual needs of the Muslim diaspora of Great Britain.

The 'Islam for Kids' initiative is part of the longstanding services of Minhaj-ul-Quran International. This Islamic Studies series was produced and developed by second and third generation British scholars, who are trained classically in the traditional Islamic sciences, alongside QTS (Qualified Teaching Status) accredited teachers. It is an indigenous and local endeavour by the UK branch of Minhaj-ul-Quran International to fulfil the educational needs of native English-speaking students.

Name: ______________________________

Class: ______________________________

Teacher: ______________________________

Islamic Studies
Textbook Level 5

Minhaj-ul-Quran International

Published by

Minhaj-ul-Quran Publications
30 Brindley Road
Manchester
M16 9HQ (UK)

Acknowledgements

Bilal Hussain, Safina Nazir, Muhammad Zeeshan Qadri, Ali Akbar, Raffiq Patel and M. Dawood Mehmood

A sincere thank you to Ajmal Khan for his assistance in the design work

ISBN: 978-1-908229-59-5

www.minhajpublications.com

www.islamforkids.org.uk

First published August 2018

Printed by Mega Printing in Turkey

The Syllabus

The 'Islam for Kids' Islamic Studies series has been split into six levels with each level corresponding to the years of the state-funded education system in the UK. It is recommended to start level one at the age of 5 when the child starts year one at primary school and to complete level 6 by the age of 11 when the child completes his or her primary school education. However, the series can be started earlier at an earlier age or later depending on the ability of the student.

The six levels have been grouped into three stages, with each stage consisting of two levels. In the first stage, which consists of levels one and two, the aim is to ease the child into understanding Islamic concepts and terminology. The purpose of this stage is not to burden the child with technical knowledge about Islam, but rather to simply instil in them a sense of Muslim identity and to explore key Islamic concepts.

Traditionally, Muslim parents have been advised to have a play-based approach with their children's learning for the first seven years and then to formally teach them for the next seven years. Following this advice, in the first two years of the syllabus, a more visual approach has been adopted with the text being kept at a minimum. This enables the content to be taught in a child-friendly manner and allows teachers and parents to make the lessons more interactive and engaging for the child.

The second stage of the syllabus begins at level three when the child reaches seven years of age. From this level onwards, a more formal approach to learning is adopted. Many of the concepts in the first stage are revisited, but instead of being largely pictorial, they are more text-based so that the key concepts can be conveyed in detail to the child and to encourage the child to start thinking about the content in more depth.

In the third stage of the syllabus, which consists of levels five and six, the series shifts to a more text-heavy approach. This is to encourage the child to learn independently and practice their key reading and comprehension skills. The content at this level increases in difficulty to engage students academically and to raise the standard of literacy and understanding of Islamic concepts.

The concepts from the previous two stages are revisited in this third stage but in much more detail. Parents and teachers alike will find this stage beneficial as reading material to help prepare in terms of subject knowledge for teaching the lessons in the earlier two stages. In this way, the three stages work together to ease the child into becoming well acquainted with Islamic terminology, concepts and values.

By the end of this syllabus, the child will have acquired the essential Islamic knowledge (*Fard `Ayn*) for them to be able to live their life as a practising Muslim. This Islamic Studies series is an excellent resource for parents to lay the foundation for their child's learning. If Allah wills, further levels will be added to this syllabus, thus enhancing the child's understanding of Islam and enabling them to become lifelong learners of the Islamic tradition.

The First Edition

In preparation of this series, authentic and reliable content was taken from the works of great scholars who represent Islamic orthodoxy. Some of the books that were consulted in the creation of the content were:

- Imam ash-Shurunbulali's *Nur al-Idah* and its commentary, *Maraqi al-Falah*
- Imam al-Laqqani's *Jawharah at-Tawhid*
- Shaykh Salih Farfur's *ar-Risalah an-Nafi`ah fi `Ilm at-Tawhid*
- Imam Ibn Hisham's *as-Sirah an-Nabawiyyah* (including its English rendition by Martin Lings)
- Imam Ibn Kathir's *al-Bidayah wa an-Nihayah*
- and the many hadith collections compiled by the founder of Minhaj-ul-Quran, Shaykh-ul-Islam Dr Muhammad Tahir-ul-Qadri

The contents of these books have been adapted for children at an age appropriate level while keeping in consideration the specific needs and requirements of Western Muslims.

We are eager to hear from the wider community and to gain feedback regarding the series. For this purpose, we have set up an email address for you to send us your feedback. You can contact us at the following address: **feedback@fmriuk.org**.

Acknowledgements

Before closing, I would like to thank my co-editors, Jawed Iqbal Tahiri and Mariam Khalid, for their commitment and assistance in helping to prepare and develop the contents of this syllabus. I would also like to thank the Series Director, Tahseen Khalid, for his great determination and support in bringing this series to fruition.

I would also like to thank Bilal Hussain for his assistance in preparing the outline of the syllabus and the Textbook Review Team (Safina Nazir, Muhammad Zeeshan Qadri, Ali Akbar, Raffiq Patel and Dawood Mehmood) for their feedback and support. A special thank you goes to Ajmal Khan for the outstanding devotion he has shown in improving and further developing the design work.

I pray to Allah that He accepts our efforts and makes it a means of salvation for us in this life and the next, and we pray that this series becomes a means of uplifting the Ummah for generations to come.

Amin bi-jahi Sayyid al-Mursalin ﷺ.

Waqas Ahmed Amin
Minhaj-ul-Quran Publications
1st Dhu al-Hijjah 1439 AH/12th August 2018 CE

Contents

Lesson 1

Belief in Allah's Existence

'Allah' is the Arabic word for God. We believe in the '**existence**' of Allah (God). This means that Allah has always been there, and He is real. Allah is so great that we cannot see Him with our eyes, touch Him with our hand or hear Him with our ears. We are unable to go to Allah directly, so how can we know Him?

We know Allah through His Prophets. Allah spoke to His Prophets and gave them His special message called '**Revelation**'. Allah does not speak directly to every person, but He sends His Prophets. The Prophets then teach their people what Allah tells them. This is how we come to know Allah (the One God), His Names, Attributes and Commandments.

Allah Gave the Prophets Miracles

Allah knew that Shaytan would misguide people and tell people not to believe in the Prophets. So, He gave the Prophets signs to tell their people that they are really Allah's Prophets. These signs are called '**miracles**'.

When people did not believe in Allah, the Prophets performed miracles to show people that they are telling them the truth. But even after seeing the miracles, some people did not want to believe; instead, they called the Prophets magicians and sorcerers. No matter how much the Prophets told them to believe in Allah they would not accept it, and they would accuse the Prophets and say that they are liars or mad.

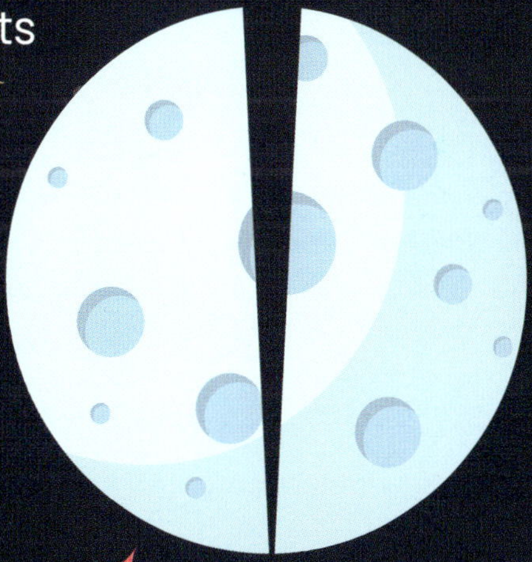

Prophet Muhammad ﷺ performed many miracles in his lifetime. Once, the leaders from the Quraysh asked the Prophet ﷺ to show them a miracle by splitting the moon in two.

"If I do it, will you believe me?" asked the Prophet ﷺ, and they all said, "Yes."

So, one night, when there was a full moon, the Prophet ﷺ gathered everyone together, and he prayed to Allah to show the disbelievers the miracle that they had asked for. As soon as the Prophet ﷺ

prayed to Allah the moon split in two. One half was over Mountain Abu Qays and the other half was over the mountain on the opposite side. The Prophet ﷺ called on the disbelievers to bear witness, but they turned away from the miracle and called it magic.

Despite seeing the many miracles of the Prophets, the disbelievers did not want to believe. Only those who submitted themselves before the Prophets in humility believed in them and accepted their message. Those who did not accept the Prophets, they disbelieved in Allah and rejected His revelation.

The Prophets Taught Us to Use Our Intellect

Allah is so sublime and perfect that we cannot see, hear or touch Him. As we cannot talk to Him directly, we need signs to remind us of Him. The greatest of Allah's signs are His Prophets, because they know Allah directly, and they tell us about Him. But other than the Prophets and Messengers, Allah has placed many other signs around us to let us know that He exists.

The Prophets used these signs to explain to us about Allah's existence and His greatness. They taught us how to use our minds properly: they explained that everything has a beginning; and if something has a beginning, it means it must have a creator, because nothing comes into existence all by itself. As this universe had a beginning, it means it also had a creator, and that creator is Allah – the One God.

Allah commanded Prophet Muhammad ﷺ to remind people of these signs, but those who close their hearts and minds to these signs will not understand them and they will not believe.

Story – Imam Abu Hanifah and the Disbelievers

A group of disbelievers wanted to debate with Imam Abu Hanifah about the existence of Allah (God). So, Imam Abu Hanifah and the disbelievers set a date for the debate.

On the day of the debate, Imam Abu Hanifah did not turn up. The disbelievers waited for a long time until they thought Imam Abu Hanifah would not come. "Imam Abu Hanifah is afraid to debate as he knows he will lose," said one of the disbelievers, "this is why he has not come."

When the disbelievers were ready to leave, suddenly Imam Abu Hanifah turned up. He apologised for being late and explained the reason.

"As I was making my way," he explained, "I found myself at the bank of the river. There were no ships to carry me across. I looked around, but I could not see anyone. As soon as I made my mind up to return home, a tree fell; it then started cutting itself into long pieces of wood. The pieces of wood then started to arrange themselves perfectly into a boat, and then the boat was floating on the water. I got onto the boat, and without there being a sailor it ferried me across to the other side of the river, and I was able to come here today."

When the disbelievers heard this, they laughed at Imam Abu Hanifah. "How silly is this story," they remarked, "how can a boat make itself without a maker and then sail across the river without a sailor?"

"You do not believe one word of my story?" asked Imam Abu Hanifah.

"Of course not! How can we believe in this nonsense?" cried the disbelievers.

Imam Abu Hanifah turned to them all and said:

"If you cannot believe a boat can make itself without a maker, how then can you believe that this whole universe and everything it contains can make itself without a creator?"

When the disbelievers heard this, they became silenced. They knew it was not possible for this universe with all its perfection and orderliness to be made all by itself. It could only have been made through an All-Powerful Creator. So, they turned to Allah in repentance and they became believers.

Lesson 2

The Importance and Benefits of Wudu'

Cleanliness is an important part of Islam. Its importance can be understood from the following words of Prophet Muhammad ﷺ. It is reported that he ﷺ said:

"Cleanliness is half of Iman (faith)." (Muslim)

The Prophet ﷺ taught us the importance of cleanliness by emphasising that only a believing person will keep his or her Wudu' (Ibn Majah). Such is the importance of Wudu' (the Ritual Ablution) that it was one of the first things Prophet Muhammad ﷺ taught his Ummah, because as Muslims, we cannot offer the five daily prayers unless we are in a state of purity (Taharah).

The Spiritual Benefits of Wudu'

There are many spiritual benefits in performing the Wudu'. Prophet Muhammad ﷺ taught us that performing the Wudu' brings light to the body parts that are washed regularly. On the Day of Judgement, Allah will bring light to the faces, arms and feet of the Muslims and this light will make the Muslims stand out from the rest of the people. The Prophet ﷺ will recognise his Ummah easily because of this light and he will help them and pray for their forgiveness. We should try to increase this light by performing the Wudu' regularly (Muslim).

Prophet Muhammad ﷺ also taught us that when we wash our hands, face, arms and feet during the Wudu', the minor sins that we commit with the eyes, hands and feet are washed away (Muslim). By performing the Wudu' correctly Allah removes our sins and raises our status in Paradise (Jannah).

Performing the Wudu' is one of the best ways to protect ourselves from Shaytan and the evil Jinn. It creates a spiritual shield around us and protects us from their bad influences. The person who stays in Wudu' regularly gets a spiritual boost and is protected from mental illnesses.

The Medical Benefits of Wudu'

As well as its many spiritual benefits, there are also medical benefits in performing the Wudu'. The way of Prophet Muhammad ﷺ is always the best way because it is the most natural way for human beings to live and it is according to the way Allah made us. In Islam, living a natural way of life is known as '**fitrah**'.

Performing the Wudu' is an important part of keeping good health because we use water to wash away germs. Water is the best and most natural way to purify ourselves. We should use water to clean our private parts after we finish from the toilet. Water does a better job of removing filth and germs than using only toilet paper. It is recommended to first wipe away the filth with tissue paper and then to use water to clean ourselves, and then to dry ourselves.

Prophet Muhammad ﷺ taught us to wash regularly throughout the day rather than washing only once or twice. Even if we are in the state of purity (Taharah), it is recommended to repeat the Wudu' again for the prayer. The Prophet ﷺ promised ten rewards to the person who does this (Abu Dawud). Performing the Wudu' when you are already in the state of purity (Taharah) has been described by some Muslim scholars as being '**light upon light**'.

Prophet Muhammad ﷺ also taught us to brush our teeth before every prayer. The Prophet ﷺ did not want to make things hard for us but he wanted his Ummah to perform the Wudu' before every prayer and to brush the teeth every time they perform the Wudu' (Ahmad). This shows us that it is recommended to brush the teeth several times throughout the day.

'Khilal' passing the fingers of one hand between the fingers of the other.

Performing the Wudu' helps to protect us against germs, which can lead to illnesses and diseases. We regularly rinse the mouth and nose because this is where the germs can enter the body easily through the air that we breathe and the food that we eat. We regularly wash the face to stop dust and germs gathering and settling on our face throughout the day. By washing the face three times, it cleans the outer part of the eyes and keeps the eyes moist so that they do not get dry and irritating.

The way that Prophet Muhammad ﷺ taught us to wash our hands and arms in the Wudu' is also being followed by doctors, surgeons and nurses working in hospitals. When Muslims wash their hands and arms in the Wudu' no part of the hand or arm can be left dry. Every part must be made wet otherwise, the Wudu' will not be complete. This is to make sure that every part is cleaned properly.

The recommended way of washing the hands according to the World Health Organisation and the NHS is by placing the palm of one hand on the back of the other hand and passing the fingers of one hand between the fingers of the other hand. Muslim scholars call this special method of washing the

hands '**khilal**', and it is performed during the Wudu'.

Doctors are also told to wash their hands, wrists and the arm up to the elbow and to run water down their forearm after washing and letting the water drip down from the elbows. This special way of washing is the same way as washing the arms in Wudu' taught to us by Prophet Muhammad ﷺ.

"Washing the arms and letting the water run down up to the elbows"

Performing the Wudu' means that we wash regularly throughout the day and this stops germs from gathering and building up. For example, our feet get fresh air when we take off our shoes and socks to wash them. During the day, our feet become sweaty and by washing them we remove the chance of an infection developing. Doing the 'khilal' on the feet also helps to remove the dirt and filth between the toes and helps in keeping them clean.

Even though more than 1400 years have passed, the method of cleanliness taught to us by Prophet Muhammad ﷺ is still advanced and more complete than anything that we have today. It is the most practical, simple and natural method, which can be practised in all times and places. Certainly, the Wudu' is a great blessing for us all.

"O believers! When (you intend) to stand for Prayer, then, (for ablution,) wash your faces and hands up to the elbows, and pass your wet hands over your heads and (also wash) your feet up to the ankles." (al-Ma'idah 5:6)

Lesson 3

Seeking Knowledge

Islam gives great importance to knowledge. The first revelation brought down by Angel Jibra'il to Prophet Muhammad ﷺ was the command to read. Prophet Adam عليه السلام was better than the angels because of his knowledge. When Allah asked the angels to give Him the names of the things, the angels were not able to do it because they did not know. But Prophet Adam عليه السلام named the things because Allah had taught him the names and this showed the angels why human beings were given a higher status. The angels recognised Adam's superiority and they fell in prostration before him.

In the Qur'an, Allah says that He raises the status of those people who believe in Him and are given knowledge (al-Mujadalah 58:11).

Importance of Seeking Knowledge

Prophet Muhammad ﷺ said, "Seeking knowledge is obligatory upon every Muslim." (Ibn Majah) Every Muslim, male and female, must seek knowledge and keep learning things during their whole life. Seeking knowledge does not stop once we finish from school; we must keep on learning and improving ourselves every day.

We seek knowledge so that we can act on what we learn, and when we act on our knowledge, our knowledge becomes a light which lights up our heart. Acting on our knowledge is one of the best ways of getting close to Allah.

Learning about Islam is one of the best types of knowledge because it brings us closer to Allah and His Prophet Muhammad ﷺ. As Muslims, we should learn all kinds of knowledge, not just knowledge about Islam. As long as the knowledge that we learn makes us better human beings and helps others. As a community, we must try our best and study hard to reach the highest level in every subject.

Respecting Teachers

One of the greatest jobs a person can do is to become a teacher. All the Prophets were teachers for their people, and teaching others and giving guidance is the main purpose of Prophethood. In the Qur'an, Allah describes Prophet Muhammad ﷺ as a teacher (al-Jumu`ah 62:2). The Prophet ﷺ also said, "I have been sent as a teacher." (Ibn Majah)

The fact that Prophet Muhammad ﷺ was sent as a teacher shows us the high status of teachers. It shows us how much we should respect and honour them. Prophet Muhammad ﷺ encouraged us to seek knowledge and to become teachers. He said, "The best among you are those who learn the Qur'an and teach it." (al-Bukhari)

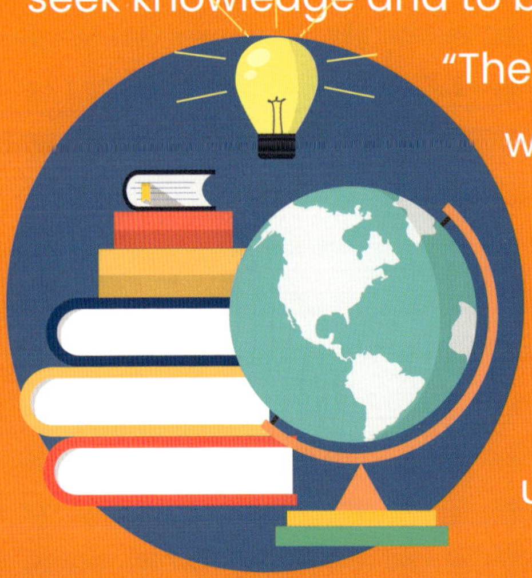

Teachers are the ones who pass knowledge on to us. If teachers did not exist, the human gift of knowledge would be lost. Children would grow up not knowing how to read or write or even how to behave properly. It is because of the efforts of our teachers that we become good people and we learn how to live on the earth properly. No wonder the animals on the earth, the birds in the sky and the fish in the sea pray for the good teacher! (at-Tirmidhi)

If we are good students, the angels will put their wings on the ground for us when we walk to our lessons, and Allah will make the world love us. If we want this great honour, then we must begin by honouring our teachers. We must be respectful to them and listen to what they say. We should show them kindness and never use bad language or be rude to them. In this way, we will grow to become better people and achieve great things in our life when we get older.

The Importance of Scholars

Those people who are given the right knowledge are chosen by Allah. Allah raises their status over others. In the Qur'an, Allah asks, "*Can the one who has knowledge and the who does not have knowledge be the same?*" (az-Zumar 39:9)

Being blessed with knowledge is a sign of Allah's kindness because it shows that Allah wants the person to be blessed with goodness. Prophet Muhammad ﷺ said, "When Allah wishes good for someone, He gives him proper understanding of the religion." (al-Bukhari)

The scholars are those people who have been given this goodness. The Prophets do not leave gold or silver coins behind for their followers. They

leave knowledge. Leaving something behind after we die is called inheritance, and knowledge is the inheritance of the Prophets. The scholars are given this inheritance and therefore they are the heirs of the Prophets (at-Tirmidhi). They pass this inheritance onto us by giving us knowledge.

We should follow the example of the angels and show respect to the people of knowledge. Showing respect to them is one of the ways of honouring the knowledge that Allah has given to them. When we have difficulty in understanding something we must go to them for help and guidance. Allah tells us to go to them when we do not have knowledge and we want to learn (an-Nahl 16:43).

How to Receive the Prophetic Inheritance?

When we want to learn Islamic knowledge, we must go to the true heirs of the Prophets. Not everyone who speaks about Islam or writes a book is a scholar. It takes a long time and many years of studying with teachers to get the Prophetic inheritance. When we want to know more about Islam we need to make sure that we go to the right people. We cannot receive Prophetic knowledge just by surfing the internet or watching programmes on T.V.!

The Prophetic inheritance is a light which is passed down from teacher to student. All the great scholars of Islam can trace their line of teachers back to Prophet Muhammad ﷺ. They have '**chains of transmission**' (**Isnad**) which explains how this Prophetic inheritance was passed on from teacher to student throughout the generations. It is a chain that connects the teacher and student back to Prophet Muhammad ﷺ. When we want to learn knowledge, we must learn it from these great scholars who have this 'chain of transmission' (Isnad).

We should not take all our knowledge from the internet because the people who write things on the internet might not give us the correct information about Islam because they might not know the correct information themselves. We should be very careful and not listen to what everyone says. Getting the Prophetic inheritance takes a long time of learning and studying, and it cannot be achieved easily. If we want to receive this blessing, we must keep the company of elder scholars and learn from them. We must be patient and spend many years listening to our elders. By doing this, we can also become the Prophetic heirs — *in sha' Allah*.

Lesson 4

Sirah: The Boycott and the Year of Sorrow

As the number of Muslims grew day by day, the Quraysh were becoming more and more irritated by the spread of Islam. Prophet Muhammad ﷺ and his followers faced increased hostility from the Quraysh.

Abu Talib, the Prophet's uncle, knew that the Quraysh would not allow the Prophet ﷺ to carry on with his mission in peace. He was scared for his nephew's safety. So, he gathered together all his family and relatives to ask them to protect the Prophet ﷺ.

Everyone, whether they were Muslim or not, agreed to Abu Talib's request. The only person who did not agree was Abu Lahab. His hatred for Islam was so intense that he was prepared to go against his own family and side with the idol worshippers instead! This was very unusual for the Arabs as it was their custom to stand by their tribe even if they did not get along with one another.

The Quraysh knew that they could not kill the Prophet ﷺ, because it would cause fighting between the different clans in the Quraysh. They decided to make things difficult for the Prophet's family and force them to give up the Prophet ﷺ. So, they decided to boycott them. They made some rules that said nobody could buy from them or sell to them and nobody could marry any man or woman from them. They hung these rules inside the Ka`bah so that no one would back down.

During these difficult years, the Prophet's family and relatives left their homes and went to a narrow passage on the border of Makkah, which came to be known as the '**Mountain Pass of Abu Talib**' (**Shi`b Abi Talib**). The Quraysh placed a blockade and did not let any food enter for the Prophet ﷺ, his family and relatives. They were suffering so much that they were forced to eat dry leaves from bushes and plants to survive.

The Muslims tried their best to help the Prophet ﷺ and his relatives. Abu Bakr, who was a rich man, spent a lot of his money on bringing food and other things through the blockade. By the end of the boycott, Abu Bakr had spent most of his money and he was no longer a rich man.

Even with this support, the Prophet's family and relatives were going through a very hard time and eventually other kind hearted people who felt sorry for them demanded that the boycott should be lifted. But the Quraysh would not listen.

The Prophet ﷺ sent his uncle Abu Talib to inform the Quraysh that Allah sent a revelation to him that said ants had eaten away the paper on which the rules were written. Abu Talib challenged the Quraysh that if what his nephew has said is not true, then he would be ready to give him up to them;

otherwise, they should end the boycott against them. The Quraysh agreed to this.

They went inside the Ka`bah and they found that the document had been eaten away by ants and nothing was left except the words: 'In Your name, O Allah.' In this way, after three difficult years, the boycott eventually came to an end, allowing the Prophet ﷺ, his family and relatives to return home in peace.

However, for the Prophet ﷺ this was not the end of his troubles. He was about to go through a very difficult and sad time in his life. His uncle Abu Talib, who was his protector and like a father to him, and Khadijah, his beloved wife and greatest friend, both died. Losing two very close and beloved people was a big loss for the Prophet ﷺ, and for this reason, this year was named **`Am al-Huzn (the Year of Sorrow)**.

The Prophet ﷺ was very sad. He lost his protector and the Quraysh continued to hate the message of Islam. So, the Prophet ﷺ decided to take his message to other places. He travelled to a place called Ta'if with his freed-slave, Zayd bin Harithah. He hoped the people of Ta'if would accept his message and support him in his mission, but they did not. The leaders of Ta'if rejected the Prophet's message saying, "If Allah sent you as a Prophet then we will tear down the cloth of the Ka`bah."

They then told young children and slaves to attack the Prophet ﷺ. They threw stones at him until his blessed body was covered in blood. There was so much blood that the Prophet's blessed sandals were stuck to the bottom of his feet. The

Prophet ﷺ left and went to a garden and sat under the shade of a tree praying to Allah for strength.

During this time, an angel from a nearby mountain came to the Prophet ﷺ and asked him permission to move the mountains and crush the people of Ta'if as a punishment for their behaviour. But the Prophet ﷺ was a '**Mercy to the All the Worlds**' and he did not give permission to the angel. Instead, he prayed for them, saying, "Perhaps Allah will make their children Muslims in the future."

While resting in the garden, a slave called `Addas met the Prophet ﷺ and gave him some water to drink and fruit to eat. The Prophet ﷺ ate the fruits saying, "In the name of Allah". `Addas looked at the

Prophet ﷺ with interest, and said, "Those words are not from this land."

"Where are you from," asked the Prophet ﷺ, "and what is your religion."

"I am a Christian from Nineveh in Iraq," `Addas replied.

"From the city of Prophet Yunus, the son of Matta," said the Prophet ﷺ.

"How do you know Yunus, the son of Matta?" asked `Addas.

"He is my brother," said the Prophet ﷺ, "he was a Prophet and I am a Prophet."

`Addas kissed the Prophet ﷺ on his head, his hands and feet, and then left.

When `Addas' master asked him about their meeting, he said, "Master, there is no one better than him on the earth. He told me things only a Prophet of Allah could know."

Lesson 5

The Witr Prayer

The Witr prayer is a three-unit prayer that we perform after the four units of the `Isha' prayer. This prayer is a **Wajib** prayer, which means it must be performed and cannot be missed. Just like a Fard prayer, if the Witr prayer is missed it must be made up at another time. Making up the prayer when it has been missed is known as '**Qada**''. The Witr prayer cannot be performed sitting down, unless a person is ill or cannot stand up because of medical reasons.

When we perform the Witr prayer, it is necessary to make our intention clearly, to offer the three units of the **Witr (Wajib)** prayer.

In the third unit (rak`ah) of the Witr prayer, we recite a special supplication (du`a) known as the **Qunut** supplication. After reciting Surat al-Fatihah and a short Surah in the Qiyam (the standing position), we raise our hands and say 'Allaahu

Akbar'. We then fold our hands again and recite the Qunut supplication before going to the Ruku` (the bowing position).

The method of performing the Witr prayer is mentioned in detail below.

How to Offer the Witr Prayer

1. Face the Qiblah and make the Niyyah to perform the three unit Witr (Wajib) prayer.

2. Perform the Takbir at-Tahrimah.

3. Perform two units of prayer as normal. In the first sitting (Qa`dah) recite only the Tashahhud.

4. Begin the third unit by performing the Qiyam (the Standing Position). Recite the Tasmiyah, then Surat al-

Fatihah followed by a short Surah.

5. Raise your hand and perform the takbir (as in step 2).

6. Folding your hands again, recite the Qunut supplication.

7. Perform the Ruku' (the Bowing Position).

8. Perform the Qawmah (the Short Standing Position).

9. Perform the Sajdah (the Prostration Position) twice with the Jalsah (the Short Sitting Position) in between.

10. Perform the Qa'dah (the Sitting Position).

Recite the Tashahhud. Then recite the Salat Ibrahimiyyah followed by a Du`a.

11. End the prayer by performing the Salam (The Ending Position).

This completes the prayer.

The Qunut Supplication

Allaah humma innaa nasta`inuka wa nastaghfiruka wa nu`minu bika wa natawakkalu alayka wa nuthni alaykal-khayr. Wa nashkuruka wa laa nakfuruka wa nakhla`u wa natruku may-yafjuruk. Allaah humma iyyaaka na`budu wa laka nusalli wa nasjudu wa ilayka nas`aa wa nahfidu wa narju rahmataka wa nakhshaa `azaabaka; innaa `azaabaka bil-kuffaari mulhiq.

اَللّٰهُمَّ إِنَّا نَسْتَعِيْنُكَ وَنَسْتَغْفِرُكَ وَنُؤْمِنُ بِكَ وَنَتَوَكَّلُ عَلَيْكَ وَنُثْنِيْ عَلَيْكَ الْخَيْرَ. وَنَشْكُرُكَ وَلَا نَكْفُرُكَ وَنَخْلَعُ وَنَتْرُكُ مَن يَّفْجُرُكَ. اَللّٰهُمَّ إِيَّاكَ نَعْبُدُ وَلَكَ نُصَلِّيْ وَنَسْجُدُ وَإِلَيْكَ نَسْعٰى وَنَحْفِدُ نَرْجُوْ رَحْمَتَكَ وَنَخْشٰى عَذَابَكَ. إِنَّ عَذَابَكَ بِالْكُفَّارِ مُلْحِقٌ

O Allah! We seek Your help and we beg for Your forgiveness. We believe in You and we rely on You and praise You. We are grateful to You and we are not ungrateful to You and we leave those who disobey You. O Allah! You alone do we worship and to You do we pray and prostrate, and we try to please You and present ourselves for Your service. We hope for Your mercy and fear Your punishment. Undoubtedly, Your severe torment is going to overtake the disbelievers.

If you do not know this supplication, then you can recite the following supplication:

Allaahumma Rabbanaa aatinaa fid-dunyaa hasanah wa fil-aakhirati hasanah waqinaa `azaaban-naar.

اَللَّهُمَّ رَبَّنَا آتِنَا فِي الدُّنْيَا حَسَنَةً وَفِي الْآخِرَةِ حَسَنَةً وَقِنَا عَذَابَ النَّارِ

O Allah, my Lord! Give me good in this life and give me good in the next life and save us from the Hellfire.

Lesson 6

The Beautiful Names of Allah

Allah has many names, but the most famous of them are 99. These 99 names are known as '**Asma' Allah al-Husna**' (The Beautiful Names of Allah). They are described as beautiful in the Qur'an: "*Allah – There is no god but Him. He has the most Beautiful Names.*" (Ta-Ha 20:8)

The Prophet ﷺ taught us that there are 99 names and has given glad tidings for the one who learns them. He said, "Allah has ninety-nine names, i.e. one-hundred less one, and whoever knows them will go to Paradise (Jannah)." (al-Bukhari)

Some of the beautiful names refer to Allah's **characteristics** and **actions** while others come as **opposite pairs.**

Allah's Characteristics

Some of the Beautiful Names that describe Allah's characteristics are:

- **AR-RAHMAN (THE MOST COMPASSIONATE) and AR-RAHIM (THE MERCIFUL):** Both of these Beautiful Names refer to Allah's mercy. Ar-Rahman refers to Allah's mercy for the believers and disbelievers in this life, while ar-Rahim refers to Allah's mercy for the believers in the next life. Ar-Rahman is a special name which belongs to Allah alone.

- **AS-SALAM (THE PERFECT/SOURCE OF PEACE):** This beautiful name refers to Allah's perfection. Allah is free from all faults and imperfections. He is a source of peace, because peace comes from Him.

- **AL-HALIM (THE LENIENT):** Allah knows everything that His creation do and say. He sees the crimes and acts of disobedience committed by them, but He does not punish them straight away. Instead, he gives everyone time to repent and ask for forgiveness.

- **AL-`AZIM (THE MAGNIFICENT):** This means Allah is the greatest. He is greater than the skies and the heavens. No one can see Allah as He cannot be seen with our two eyes. Nothing can encompass Allah due to His greatness and magnificence.

- **AL-`ALIYY (THE SUBLIME):** Allah is the sublime. This means that He is the greatest and that there is none greater than Him. Everyone is inferior to Allah and no one is equal to Him.

- **AL-KARIM (THE GENEROUS):** Allah is the most generous. If He promises His servants something, He fulfils it. When He gifts His servants, He gives them more than they deserve, and He gives without any limits.

- **AL-HAKIM (THE WISE):** Allah knows what is best. He knows the reality of everything. He is the most-wise. Everything Allah does is for the best because no one has better understanding than Him.

- **AL-WADUD (THE LOVING):** Allah loves goodness for His creation, and He always does what is best for them. He praises the good actions of His servants and rewards them.
- **AL-WALI (THE PROTECTING FRIEND):** Only Allah is the true helper. He is the protector of His friends and servants. He defends His friends and protects them from their enemies.

Allah's Actions

Some of the Beautiful Names that describe Allah's actions are:

- **AL-KHALIQ (THE CREATOR):** Allah is the creator of everything. No one can create, because to create you must bring something that does not exist into existence. Only Allah can make things from nothing. All the raw material humans use to make things are created by Allah; without them humans cannot make anything.

- **AL-MUSAWWIR (THE FASHIONER):** Allah is the creator of shape and forms. Human beings cannot create new shapes by themselves. They can only copy the shapes and forms that are already created by Allah. Whatever exists within Allah's creation, human beings copy it and then change it to something else using the imagination bestowed on them by Allah.

- **AL-WAHHAB (THE BESTOWER):** Allah gives gifts and bestows favours to His creation without any need or desire to get anything in return. He gives freely and without limits.

- **AR-RAZZAQ (THE PROVIDER):** Allah is the creator of food and water. Allah creates ways for our survival and existence. Food, water and air are Allah's creations, and they are the ways that Allah has provided for us to satisfy our needs.

- **AL-FATTAH (THE SOLVER):** Allah is the One Who solves all our problems and removes our difficulties. Allah creates new opportunities for us and if we cannot find a way out He creates a way for us.

- **AL-GHAFUR (THE FORGIVER):** Allah is the One Who forgives. His forgiveness is widespread and complete; it includes everyone, and it reaches the greatest levels of forgiveness.

- **ASH-SHAKUR (THE APPRECIATIVE):** Allah gives great rewards for small acts of kindness and virtue. For a single good deed, He gives at least ten rewards, and He increases the reward as He wills without any limits.

- **AR-RAQIB (THE WATCHFUL):** Allah looks after everyone and He is aware of anything that takes place. He guards His creation and takes care of everything.

- **AL-MUJIB (THE RESPONDER):** Allah is the One Who responds to everyone's prayers. He accepts prayers and fulfils the requests of everyone who calls onto Him.
- **AL-MUNTAQIM (THE PUNISHER):** Allah questions the sinners and evildoers and holds them responsible for their actions. He does not let anyone who does injustice to get away with their crime. When Allah punishes someone, His punishment is swift and severe.

Opposite Pairs

Some of the Beautiful Names that come as opposite pairs are:

- **AL-QABID (THE RESTRICTOR) and AL-BASIT (THE EXPANDER):** Allah is the One Who increases provision (e.g. food and water) and He limits them as well.

- **AL-MU`IZZ (THE HONOURER) and AL-MUZILL (THE HUMILIATOR):** Allah gives power and authority to whoever He wills, and He takes it away from whoever He wills.

- **AL-MUHYI (THE GIVER OF LIFE) and AL-MUMIT (THE GIVER OF DEATH):** Allah is the Master of life and death. No one lives or dies except by His will.

- **AL-MUQADDIM (THE ADVANCER) and AL-MU`AKKHIR (THE DELAYER):** Allah brings forward whoever He wills, and He pushes back whoever He wills.

- **AN-NAFI` (THE MASTER OF BENEFIT) and AD-DARR (THE MASTER OF HARM):** All good and bad comes from Allah. Allah is the owner of benefit and harm. Nothing can bring us any benefit or harm except if Allah wills it.

Lesson 7

Prophet Yusuf عليه السلام (Part One)

One night, Prophet Yusuf عليه السلام saw eleven planets, the sun and the moon all bowing down to him in a dream. In the morning, he woke up excited. He went straight to his father Prophet Ya`qub عليه السلام and told him about his dream. Prophet Ya`qub عليه السلام said to him, “My dear son, do not tell your brothers about this dream.”

Prophet Yusuf عليه السلام had eleven brothers. He and his younger brother Binyamin were the youngest. Prophet Ya`qub عليه السلام was worried that if he told his brothers about his dream they would get jealous of him and would try to hurt him. He wanted to protect Prophet Yusuf عليه السلام from his older brothers. So, he told him to keep quiet about the dream. He explained to his son that Allah has chosen him to be a Prophet, like his father and grandfathers, and that He will give Him special knowledge and the ability to understand dreams.

Prophet Ya`qub عليه السلام loved Prophet Yusuf عليه السلام a lot. He would never let him out of his sight. This made Prophet Yusuf's older brothers jealous. They said, "Yusuf and his younger brother are more beloved to our father than us, even though we are strong."

Their jealousy made them angry, so they decided to kill Prophet Yusuf عليه السلام. But the eldest brother among them said, "No! Don't kill Yusuf. Why not just throw him in a well?" The brothers all agreed to this idea and they decided to work together on this plan.

When the unfortunate day came, they went to their father and asked him to let Prophet Yusuf عليه السلام go with them. At first their father did not agree; fearing something bad might happen to him. He said, "I am afraid that a wolf might come and kill him." The brothers kept on persuading their father to let Prophet Yusuf عليه السلام go with them, until their father finally agreed.

Once the brothers reached a place faraway, they got hold of Prophet Yusuf عليه السلام and threw him down a well. While Prophet Yusuf عليه السلام was in the dark well, Allah told him not to worry and promised him that one day he would get the chance to tell his brothers what they did to him.

The brothers went back to their father with tears rolling down their cheeks.

Earlier, they had killed a sheep and put its blood on Prophet Yusuf's shirt. They showed the shirt to their father, saying that a wolf killed Prophet Yusuf عليه السلام while they were busy working. But their father did not believe them. Instead, he turned to Allah for help and chose to remain patient in this difficult situation.

While Prophet Yusuf عليه السلام was in the well, a caravan came and found him there. They took

him out, and exclaimed, "Good news! Here is a boy." They took Prophet Yusuf عليه السلام with them to Egypt and sold him for a few silver coins.

The 'Aziz of Egypt bought Prophet Yusuf عليه السلام. The 'Aziz was one of the noble men, who worked as the finance minister in the kingdom. When he brought Prophet Yusuf عليه السلام to his palace, he said to his wife Zulaykha, "Make his stay comfortable. Maybe we might benefit from him or take him as a son." In this way, Allah placed Prophet Yusuf عليه السلام in an honourable household.

Prophet Yusuf عليه السلام grew to become a very beautiful and handsome young man. His face shone like the bright moon. He had such good manners that everyone around him loved him greatly. He spoke the truth, and everyone admired him very much. Zulaykha, the wife of

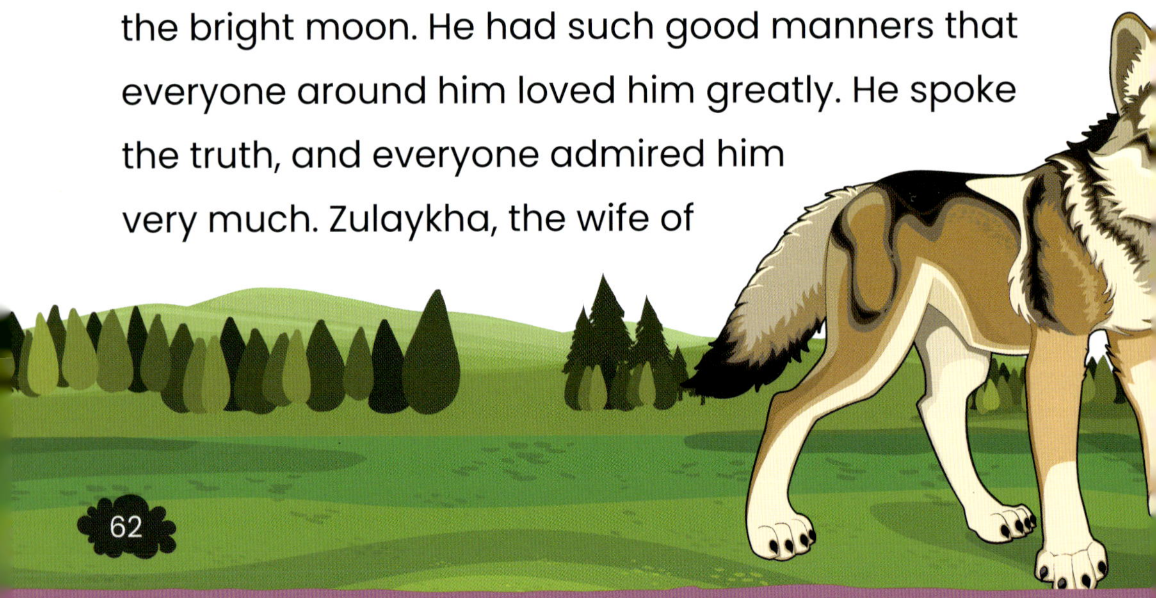

`Aziz, loved Prophet Yusuf عليه السلام very much. She wanted him all to herself. So, she thought of a plan to trap Prophet Yusuf عليه السلام.

One day, she called Prophet Yusuf عليه السلام to her room. As soon as Prophet Yusuf عليه السلام entered the room, she shut the door behind him and said, "Come here." Prophet Yusuf عليه السلام asked for Allah's protection and he told her that her husband was his master and he has honoured him, and he will not do anything wrong to betray his trust.

Prophet Yusuf عليه السلام ran for the door, but Zulaykha caught the back of his shirt, which she ripped off. As they reached for the door they found `Aziz standing there. Embarrassed at the situation, Zulaykha said, "What is the punishment for the one who wishes to do wrong to your wife?"

Prophet Yusuf عليه السلام denied that he did anything wrong. So, to work out who was to blame, a person suggested that if his shirt is ripped from the front, it means he was the one to blame; but if it is ripped from the back, it was her.

When they looked at his shirt, they saw it was ripped from the back. They understood that Prophet Yusuf عليه السلام was speaking the truth, and that Zulaykha was in the wrong.

The women friends of Zulaykha started making fun of her. So, she invited all of them to her house and gave each one a knife to cut their fruit with. She then told Prophet Yusuf عليه السلام to enter the room. As soon as the women saw him, they marvelled at Prophet Yusuf's beauty. They thought he was an angel. They were so amazed by him that they forget they had knives in their hands. They continued cutting through the fruit, and even cut their fingers without realising it.

Zulaykha seeing that the women were captivated by Yusuf's beauty, told them that if Prophet Yusuf عليه السلام did not listen to her, he would be thrown in prison. Prophet Yusuf عليه السلام asked Allah for His protection and said he would rather go to prison than to listen to Zulaykha.

Allah accepted his prayer. Despite knowing Prophet Yusuf عليه السلام was innocent, the `Aziz and the other noble men of Egypt decided to put Prophet Yusuf عليه السلام in prison for some time, so that people would stop gossiping.

Lesson 8

Helping Others (Part One)

Islam is not just a religion; it is **a complete way of life (Din)**. A religion only tells us how to worship God and how to be a spiritual person. But a complete way of life (Din) is more than just worshipping God and living as a spiritual person; it is about knowing what God wants from us in every moment of our life and following God's rules in every part of our life.

Being a true Muslim does not mean that we only worship Allah and practise the five pillars of Islam. Being a true Muslim means that we also fulfil the rights of Allah's creation. As Muslims, we must fulfil both the rights of Allah and the rights of people. These two rights are known as **'huquq Allah'** (the **rights of Allah**) and **'huquq al-`ibad'** (**the rights of Allah's creation**). These rights tell us how we should treat other people.

Islam gives as much importance to treating others well as it does to praying five times a day and fasting in the month of Ramadan. If a Muslim prays five times a day but he or she treats others badly, then that person's prayers will not help them on the Day of Judgement. All of that person's prayers will be given to the people he or she hurt and was nasty to. Allah does not care for the worship of a person who does not care about other people.

Importance of Good Character

Having good behaviour and manners is very important in Islam. It is just as important as praying.

Allah says in the Qur'an that Prophet Muhammad ﷺ was sent as a **'Mercy for all the Worlds'** (al-Anbiya' 21:107). The Prophet's mercy is for everyone, including Muslims, non-Muslims and even animals. The Prophet ﷺ would treat everyone kindly and look after everybody. Even if his enemy came to him for help, he would help them and treat them with kindness.

Prophet Muhammad ﷺ said that he was sent to show us the best character (Ahmad). He showed us the real meaning of good character through his manner and behaviour. One of the main reasons that Allah sent Prophet Muhammad ﷺ to us was that we could perfect our good character. This shows us the importance of good character in Islam.

Prophet Muhammad ﷺ wanted Muslims to be kind and helpful to others. He explained that the best Muslim is the one who is best in his or her manners and character (al-Bukhari). The Prophet ﷺ loves those people the most whose character and morals are good. He said that the people who will be the closest to him on the Day of Judgement will be those who have good morals and character (at-Tirmidhi).

Why We Need Good Character?

Having a good character, such as being kind and helpful to others, is one of the best kinds of worship, because it is one of the things that Allah rewards the most. Prophet Muhammad ﷺ said that the person who has good character reaches the same status as the person who fasts throughout the day and prays throughout the night (Abu Dawud).

Some people think that as long as they are praying and fasting, they can treat others badly and get away with their bad behaviour. This thinking is absolutely wrong. The Prophet ﷺ said that the perfect Muslim is one who is the best in character and the kindest to his family (at-Tirmidhi).

If a Muslim follows all the practices of Islam such as praying, reading the Qur'an, dressing properly etc. but he or she is not good to other people and to their family, then that person's Islam is incomplete, and he or she is not a perfect Muslim.

We should never belittle the importance of having a good character in Islam because it is highly rewarded by Allah. For example, on the Day of Judgement, when Allah will weigh our deeds on the scale, good character will weigh heavily on the side of our good deeds (at-Tirmidhi). Also, Allah has made the Hellfire forbidden for a person who is kind, helpful and soft in his character and behaviour (Ahmad).

Having good behaviour, character and manners is something that we must practise all the time, no matter who we meet. Every Muslim must always work to improve his or her behaviour and to become a better person. A person cannot become better in their character until he or she starts to think about others first. So, we should always be thoughtful and kind to everyone we meet.

The Importance of Helping Others

Being helpful is a very good deed. As Muslims, we must help people if they are in trouble or in need. The Qur'an tells us to help each other in doing good deeds and not to help someone in doing bad deeds (al-Ma'idah 5:2). Prophet Muhammad ﷺ, who is the best of all creation, also told us that the person who helps people in need is the best person (at-Tabarani). So, if we want to please Allah and reach the highest levels in Paradise (Jannah), then we must try our best to help other people, whether they are Muslim or not.

When we help others for the sake of Allah, we should remember that we are also helping ourselves. Prophet Muhammad ﷺ explained that when a person helps someone in a time of need, Allah will be there for that person when he is in need (Muslim). As we all need Allah, the best way to get Allah's help is to help others.

If we want Allah to help us, then we must help others, even if it is something as simple as carrying someone's shopping or opening the door for them.

Prophet Muhammad ﷺ said that Allah will keep on helping us as long as we are helping others (Muslim). If we spend our whole life trying to make the world around us a better place by helping others in whatever way that we can, then we will be highly rewarded by Allah.

Prophet Muhammad ﷺ told us that when we remove a difficulty from someone, Allah will remove a difficulty from us on the Day of Judgement (al-Bukhari). This is why we should never look down at the importance of helping others or think that it is a small thing. Allah explains in the Qur'an that the reward of good cannot be anything but good (ar-Rahman 55:60). If we do good to others, it will never go to waste because Allah will always remember the good that we have done, and in one way or another, He will return that good to us in this life and the next life.

Lesson 9

Sirah: The Night Journey and the Ascension to Heaven

Prophet Muhammad ﷺ was going through the most difficult times of his Prophetic mission. He lost his uncle Abu Talib and his beloved wife Khadijah, and he was turned away by the people of Ta'if.

Allah wanted to make the heart of His Prophet ﷺ stronger, so He honoured him with a unique and very special gift that had not been given to anyone else before him.

The Night Journey (al-Isra')

One night, while the Prophet ﷺ was sleeping near the Ka`bah, Angel Jibra'il came to him and woke him up. He brought with him a white beast that looked like a small horse with wings. This heavenly horse was called '**al-Buraq**', which means 'multiple lightening' in Arabic, and it was so fast that every step it took, it could reach the furthest point that the eye can see.

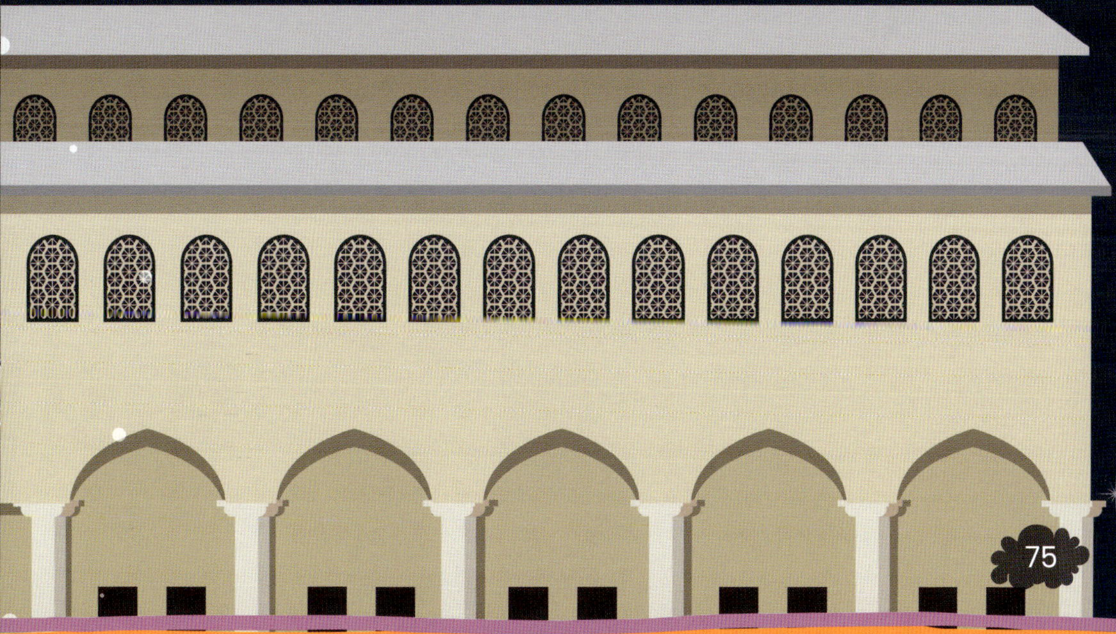

When the Prophet ﷺ went near the Buraq, it became fidgety because it was so happy that the Prophet ﷺ would be riding on him. However, Angel Jibra'il told Buraq off for this behaviour. "Do you not have any shame, O Buraq?" Jibra'il said, "what are you doing? By Allah, no servant of Allah more honourable than Muhammad has ever ridden on you."

When the Prophet ﷺ rode on the Buraq, it travelled at the speed of light. The Prophet ﷺ went to '**al-Masjid al-Aqsa**' (the Furthest Mosque) in the holy city of Jerusalem, and on the way there, he saw Prophet Musa عليه السلام standing in his grave praying. There was a gathering of the Prophets at al-Masjid al-Aqsa, and it included Prophets Ibrahim, Musa and `Isa (peace be upon them all), among many others.

The Prophets were getting ready to pray and they wanted someone to lead

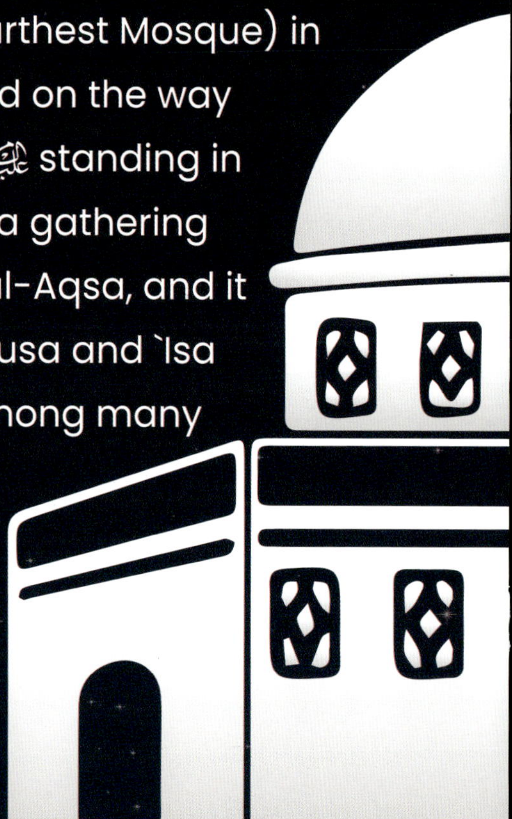

them in the prayer. But who would be the Imam to lead them? It was an easy decision: Prophet Muhammad ﷺ would lead the prayer! This decision showed the Prophet's status as the Imam and the leader of all the Prophets.

After leading the Prophets in prayer, two cups were brought before Prophet Muhammad ﷺ; one containing milk and the other wine. The Prophet ﷺ took the cup of milk and drank from it. Seeing this, Angel Jibra'il said, "You have been guided and you have guided your Ummah, O Muhammad!"

The Ascension to Heaven (al-Mi`raj)

After this great meeting, the Prophet ﷺ rode the Buraq again, but this time the Buraq started flying upwards and travelled to the heavens to a place outside of this universe. When they reached the gates of

Heaven, Angel Jibra'il asked for it to be opened, and it was opened for him. Every time they passed a group of angels, they would ask, "O Jibra'il, who is this?" And Jibra'il would reply, "Muhammad." The angels would greet them with pleasant and smiling faces.

In the heavens, the Prophet ﷺ met many of the Prophets who he led in prayer in al-Masjid al-Aqsa. On the first heaven, he met Prophet Adam عليه السلام. They greeted each other. The Prophet ﷺ then went up to the second heaven and met Prophet Yahya عليه السلام and Prophet `Isa عليه السلام. In the third heaven, he met Prophet Yusuf عليه السلام, in the fourth heaven, he met Prophet Idris عليه السلام, and in the fifth heaven, he met Prophet Harun عليه السلام. They all greeted him and said that they believe in his Prophethood.

On the sixth heaven, Prophet Muhammad ﷺ met Prophet Musa عليه السلام. When the Prophet ﷺ was about to leave, Prophet Musa عليه السلام started crying. The Prophet ﷺ asked him the reason for this. Prophet

Musa عليه السلام said, "I am lucky to meet a man who was sent after me as a Messenger of Allah who was more able to lead his people than me."

The Prophet ﷺ then went up to the seventh heaven. There he met his great grandfather, Prophet Ibrahim عليه السلام. He was shown **al-Bayt al-Ma`mur**, which is like the Ka`bah, where the Tawaf is performed by angels. Seventy thousand angels perform the Tawaf at any one time. Every time an angel performs the Tawaf of al-Bayt al-Ma`mur, it is not allowed to return to it until the Day of Judgement.

After the seventh heaven, the Prophet ﷺ was taken to '**Sidrat al-Muntaha**' (the Lote Tree of the Furthermost End). This is the point where every knower's knowledge comes to an end. Even the angels and Prophets do not know what is past this point, because everything past this point is a mystery and a secret.

It was here, where time and space came to an end, that the Prophet ﷺ saw the Divine Presence and was the closest to Allah. Allah revealed to the Prophet ﷺ whatever He willed, and He gave fifty prayers as a gift to the Prophet's Ummah.

The Obligation of the Five Daily Prayers

When the Prophet ﷺ was returning from his meeting with Allah, he met Prophet Musa عليه السلام who told the Prophet ﷺ that his followers would not be able to perform fifty prayers every day. He asked him to go back and get them reduced. So, the Prophet ﷺ did this, and Allah reduced the number of prayers. Each time the Prophet ﷺ returned, Prophet Musa عليه السلام would ask him to go back and ask Allah to reduce the number of prayers again.

The Prophet ﷺ kept on returning to Allah until the prayers were reduced to five. Again, when he returned, Prophet Musa عليه السلام told him to ask Allah to reduce them further, but the Prophet ﷺ said, "I have returned from my Lord and I have asked Him until I am ashamed. I will not go back again." And so, the Prophet ﷺ returned to the earth with the gift of five prayers a day. Allah revealed to the Prophet ﷺ that whoever offers the five daily prayers it will be the same as offering fifty prayers.

A Test for the Muslims

After receiving the gift of the five daily prayers, the Prophet ﷺ made his way back to the earth. He came down in Jerusalem at the Rock, the same place from where he first went up to the heavens. He made his way back to Makkah on the Buraq and saw groups of people on their way home.

When the Prophet ﷺ reached Makkah, he told everyone about his miraculous journey, but many people did not believe him. The disbelievers laughed at the Prophet ﷺ and teased him. They said that even a child knows that you cannot go to Jerusalem and back in one night, because the journey would take months.

The people who had weak faith became unsure if the Prophet's message was true or not. The idol worshippers thought that they had won because they thought that no one would believe such a thing.

They quickly went up to Abu Bakr as-Siddiq and said, "Your friend Muhammad believes that he went to Jerusalem and back again in one night. What do you think of him now?"

"You are lying!" replied Abu Bakr as-Siddiq.

When they convinced him that the Prophet ﷺ did say this, Abu Bakr as-Siddiq replied, "If he says it, then it is the truth, and what is so surprising about it? I believe in him when he says that revelation comes to Him from the heavens, and I know that he does not tell lies."

After telling them this, Abu Bakr as-Siddiq went around the Ka`bah and announced to the people,

"If Muhammad has said it, then it is true!" For this reason, Abu Bakr was given the name '**as-Siddiq**' (**the Verifier of the Truth**).

To prove that he was telling the truth to the Quraysh, the Prophet ﷺ told them about the groups of people that were on their way back to Makkah. He told the Quraysh of their exact location and the time it would take for them to return.

When the people returned exactly at the time described by the Prophet ﷺ, it showed that he was telling the truth. Those Muslims, who were weak in their faith, who become unsure of the Prophet's message were confident again and believed him. The truth of the Prophet's words showed them that their Prophet was speaking the truth.

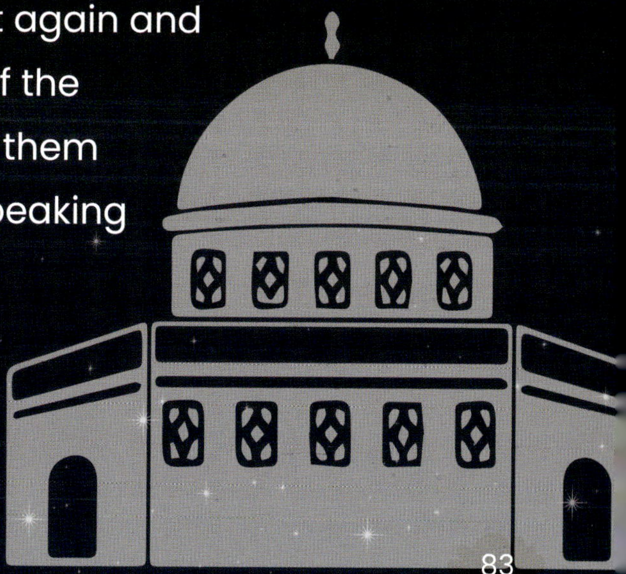

Lesson 10

Prophet Yusuf عليه السلام (Part Two)

While Prophet Yusuf عليه السلام was in prison, two men also entered the prison. One night, the two prisoners had a dream. One of them saw himself pressing grapes and making wine. The second man saw bread on his head and birds picking on it. They wanted to know the meaning of their dreams.

Prophet Yusuf عليه السلام told the first man that he would once again serve the king and he will be freed. As for the second man, he told him he would be crucified and that the judgement has been passed to kill him. The one who was to be freed, Prophet Yusuf عليه السلام asked him to mention him to the king, so that he may also be freed, but Shaytan made him forget about his promise.

As time passed, one night the king had a dream. He saw seven fat cows being eaten by seven skinny cows, and seven green ears of corn and seven dry ears of corn. When he woke up, he asked his advisors the meaning of this dream, but none of them could interpret it. They told the king it was a confused dream, but the king was not satisfied with this.

The man who was freed from prison and now served the king, suddenly remembered Prophet Yusuf عليه السلام. He promised the king to get an interpretation for the dream.

Prophet Yusuf عليه السلام told the former prisoner that the seven fat cows symbolised seven years of richness while the seven skinny cows symbolised seven years of famine and having no rain for the crops to grow. In those seven years of no rain, they would eat from the grains they stored from the previous seven years.

When the king heard this interpretation, he was pleased with Prophet Yusuf عليه السلام. He invited him to the palace, but Prophet Yusuf عليه السلام refused. He did not want to leave prison, until he was cleared of all the wrong charges against him. So, the king called all the women to testify before him, and they all told the king that Prophet Yusuf عليه السلام was innocent.

Prophet Yusuf عليه السلام was freed from jail and the king appointed him as his advisor and made him in charge of the treasures of the land. Prophet Yusuf عليه السلام agreed to this, and this is how Allah put him in a position of authority and power and gave him much honour.

As Prophet Yusuf عليه السلام forewarned, the seven years of famine did come to Egypt. But Prophet Yusuf عليه السلام with his prophetic intelligence successfully managed the stores of grain and helped the people to get through the difficult days.

During those days, Prophet Yusuf's brothers came to Egypt in the hope to receive grain. When they came to the royal palace, Prophet Yusuf ﷺ recognised them immediately, but they did not recognise him.

He asked them about their family, and they told him that their younger brother Binyamin was still in Palestine with their father. Prophet Yusuf ﷺ told them to bring Binyamin with them next time, otherwise he would not give them any grain the next time they came. They agreed to his request and they asked permission to leave. Before giving them their sacks of grain, Prophet Yusuf ﷺ told his servants to return their money and put it inside their sacks.

The brothers, upon returning home, told their father about their meeting with the noble Egyptian lord and his request to have Binyamin come with them the following year. Prophet Ya`qub ﷺ saddened by his loss was reluctant, for he did not trust his sons with Binyamin after what happened with Yusuf ﷺ.

When the brothers opened their sacks, to their surprise they found the money in there. They turned to their father and promised to take good care of Binyamin and to not let any harm reach him. In the end, Prophet Ya`qub ﷺ reluctantly agreed and took a sincere promise from them to take care of Binyamin.

When they entered Egypt, they entered through different gates to not bring any attention to themselves. When they came to Prophet Yusuf ﷺ he told them to sit with him, giving the seat next to him to his younger brother Binyamin. As they were sitting, he quietly told Binyamin that he was Yusuf, his older brother! He told him not to worry and to place full trust in Allah.

As the brothers were about to leave Egypt, a palace guard came running out and told them to stop. He accused the brothers of stealing. They did not know that Prophet Yusuf ﷺ had put the king's cup in Binyamin's sack. When they found the cup in his sack, the palace guards held Binyamin as a prisoner.

Prophet Yusuf ﷺ could not have kept Binyamin behind with him in any other way according to the Egyptian law. That is why he did this. Allah revealed this plan to Prophet Yusuf ﷺ and taught him how to complete it properly.

When the palace guards found the king's cup in Binyamin's sack, the brothers became very worried. They had promised their father to look after their younger brother and not let any harm come to him, but now Binyamin was taken as a prisoner. They pleaded to the king to let Binyamin go, or to let one of them take his place, but the king would not listen to their plea.

Seeing that they could not convince the king to change his decision, they returned to their father, except the eldest who decided to stay behind. They told Prophet Ya`qub ﷺ what had happened, but Prophet Ya`qub ﷺ remained patient and only prayed to Allah for help.

Prophet Ya`qub عليه السلام told them to return to Egypt and get some news about Binyamin. So, they went back to Egypt, and they begged Prophet Yusuf عليه السلام for mercy and to let Binyamin go, as their father was an old man and they were facing many difficulties.

Feeling sorry for them, Prophet Yusuf عليه السلام turned to them and said, “Do you remember what you did to Yusuf and his brother?”

The brothers were taken aback and stunned at this question, they asked, “Are you really Yusuf?”

“Yes,” Prophet Yusuf عليه السلام replied, “I am Yusuf and here is my brother. Indeed, Allah is kind to us and does not waste the reward of those who do good deeds.”

Ashamed of themselves, they cried, “Allah has certainly raised you above us and we alone are the sinners.”

Prophet Yusuf عليه السلام was kind and honourable so he

forgave his brothers. "No blame lies on you today," he said, "May Allah grant you His forgiveness."

He then gave his shirt to them and told them to put it over their father's face, because he lost his eyesight due to his grief. He then commanded his brothers to return to Egypt and to go back to their father.

When the brothers were approaching their home, Prophet Ya`qub عليه السلام could smell the fragrance of Prophet Yusuf عليه السلام from his shirt, but his family did not believe him. When the brothers arrived home, they put the shirt over his face and at once his eyesight returned. They asked their father for forgiveness and he prayed for their forgiveness.

They all then went to Egypt. Prophet Yusuf عليه السلام welcomed them and he seated his parents next to him. All of his brothers fell on the floor in prostration to him. Seeing this, Prophet Yusuf عليه السلام said to Prophet Ya`qub عليه السلام, "O father, this is the meaning of the dream that I had seen long ago."

Lesson 11

Prophets: Their Important Characteristics

The Prophets and Messengers are the greatest human beings. Throughout history, Allah sent Prophets and Messengers to different nations and tribes. Allah did not have to send us Prophets and Messengers, but out of His mercy and generosity, He sent them to us for our guidance.

A **Prophet** is a male human being who Allah speaks to. A **Messenger** is also a Prophet, but he has the extra duty of passing on Allah's message to his people. We must believe in all the Prophets and not treat them differently, i.e. we are not allowed to believe in some and not in others.

The Prophets and Messengers all have special qualities and good behaviour, but we must believe they had four important characteristics. These four characteristics are: truthfulness, sinlessness, intelligence and passing on Allah's message.

The First Characteristic: Truthfulness

The Prophets and Messengers only speak the truth, and they cannot lie purposefully or forgetfully. They are trustworthy in their duties and they cannot mislead or misguide their followers. They pass on Allah's message exactly as they are commanded to do so, and they do not spread falsehood about Allah and His message.

Before accepting Islam, `Abd Allah bin Salam was a respected Rabbi among the Jews of Madinah. Describing his meeting with the Prophet ﷺ, `Abd Allah bin Salam said, "When I looked at the face of the Prophet, I knew his face was not the face of a liar." (Ibn Abi Shaybah)

Abu Sufyan was one of the chiefs of the Quraysh. On one occasion, before he accepted Islam, he met the Byzantine ruler Heraclius. Heraclius asked Abu Sufyan about the Prophet ﷺ, "Did you ever accuse him of lying before he claimed Prophethood?" "No," replied Abu Sufyan. Hearing his reply, Heraclius said, "I asked you this question because, if he does not lie about others, then he could not lie about Allah." (al-Bukhari)

The Second Characteristic: Sinlessness

The Prophets and Messengers are sinless. They cannot commit any small or big sin, before or after their announcement of Prophethood. Even before they received the revelation from Allah, no Prophet ever disbelieved in Allah; they were true and perfect believers from the moment that they were born.

Allah has protected His Prophet and Messengers from sin. They cannot disobey Allah inwardly or outwardly. They cannot commit outward sins, such as stealing, gambling or swearing, nor can they commit inward sins, such as hatred, jealousy or showing off. They are the best human beings,

who are the perfect examples of obedience and submission to Allah.

Before announcing his Prophethood, Prophet Muhammad ﷺ was known among his people as '**as-Sadiq**' (the truthful) and '**al-Amin**' (the trustworthy). He was famous among his people for good character. Because of this, Lady Khadijah wanted him to trade on her behalf in Syria and the Quraysh were pleased to make the Prophet ﷺ their judge in the matter of restoring the Black Stone to the Ka`bah.

The idol worshippers of Makkah, who had not accepted Islam yet, would trust their belongings to the Prophet ﷺ because they could not find anyone more reliable or trustworthy than him. Despite their anger and hate towards Islam, the Prophet ﷺ would take care of their belongings and did not cheat them or break their trust.

The Third Characteristic: Intelligence

Allah blessed the Prophets and Messengers with high levels of intelligence. They were very clever and smart so that they were able to spread the message of Allah in the best way. They were intelligent and clever in arguing with the disbelievers when they said false things about Allah.

When Prophet Ibrahim عليه السلام stood before Nimrud, Nimrud asked him, “Who is your Lord?”

"My Lord is the One Who gives life and death," Prophet Ibrahim عليه السلام said to him.

"I give life and death," said the king. He then brought two prisoners. The one who was supposed to be killed, he ordered him to be freed believing that he gave him life; and the one who was supposed to be freed, he ordered him to be killed, believing that he gave him death.

Seeing how foolish and unwise the king was, Prophet Ibrahim عليه السلام said, "My Lord is He Who brings the sun from the east, so why don't you bring it from the west?"

When the king heard this, he became speechless. Prophet Ibrahim عليه السلام through being smart and using his intelligence showed the king that he was wrong and silenced him.

The Fourth Characteristic: Passing on Allah's Message

The Prophets and Messengers are Allah's truthful and trustworthy servants. Whatever Allah orders them, they put it into action and they never disobey Allah. Allah blessed the Prophets and Messengers with His special message, known as '**Revelation**', and He commanded them to carry that message to their people. The Prophets and Messengers passed on whatever Allah ordered them to and they did not miss out anything.

In the life of Prophet Muhammad ﷺ, we see examples of how the Prophet ﷺ worked hard to tell people about Allah's commands. The Prophet ﷺ called people to Islam day and night. He worked tirelessly to invite all the Arabs to Islam, and eventually after much struggle, they all accepted Islam and became Muslims.

After the success of Islam in Arabia, the Prophet ﷺ called on the different nations to follow his message. He sent letters to the Byzantine, Persian,

Egyptian and Abyssinian rulers and invited them to Islam. People from different nations and tribes began to accept Islam, and after the Prophet ﷺ passed away, people kept on accepting Islam. Today we see Muslims all over the world that belong to different ethnicities, nationalities and races, all one and united as a single community of believers, known as the Ummah.

Lesson 12

The Funeral Prayer

Death is a significant part of human life. The Qur'an tells us that every soul will taste death (Al `Imran 3:185). Prophet Muhammad ﷺ taught us what to do when a person dies. Some of those things are as follows:

- We wash the body of the deceased. This washing of the body is called '**ghusl**'.
- We apply a chemical called 'camphor' to the deceased's body. Applying this chemical is known as '**tahnit**' or '**hunut**'.
- We put a burial shroud on the deceased. This burial shroud is known as '**kafan**'. It is white in colour and it covers the whole body of the deceased.

- We read the funeral prayer, and this is known as '**Salat al-Janazah**'.
- We bury the deceased in the grave. Burying the deceased is known as '**dafan**'.

How to Offer the Salat al-Janazah

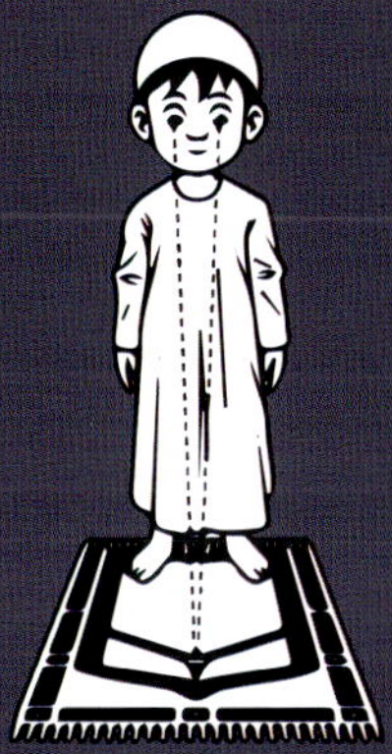

After washing the deceased's body and putting on their burial shroud, we perform the Salat al-Janazah (funeral prayer) for the deceased. This is a special prayer in which there is no Ruku` (Bowing Position), Sajdah (Prostration Position) or Qa`dah (Sitting Position). The whole prayer is performed standing up. There is no Adhan or Iqamah for this prayer. When we perform it, we must be in a state of purity (Taharah).

Unlike the five daily prayers, there is no recitation from the Qur'an in the Janazah prayer or Tashahhud (Bearing Witness). Instead, we recite the Thana` (Praise of Allah), the Salat Ibrahimiyya (Abrahamic Salutation) and the Du`a for the deceased. We also recite the Takbir (saying 'Allaahu Akbar') four times. We raise our hands the first time we say Takbir and we do not raise them the other three times it is recited.

The method of performing the Salat al-Janazah (funeral prayer) is as follows:

1. Perform the Niyyah for the Janazah prayer.

2. Perform the Takbir at-Tahrima.

3. Perform the Qiyam (the Standing Position) and recite the Thana' (Praise of Allah) with the additional words '*wa jalla thanaa'uka*'.

4. Recite the Takbir (Allaahu Akbar) without raising your hands.

5. Recite the Salat Ibrahimiyya (Abrahamic Salutation) [the same as you do in the Qa`dah (Sitting Position) in the five daily prayers].

6. Perform the Takbir (Allaahu Akbar) without raising your hands.

7. Recite the Du`a for the deceased person.

8. Perform the Takbir (Allaahu Akbar) without raising your hands.

9. Make the Salam (the Ending Position) while in the Qiyam (the Standing Position), turning the head first to the right then to the left.

This completes the funeral prayer (Salat al-Janazah).

The Niyyah (Intention)

Nawaytu 'an usalliya salaat al-janaazah `ala'l-mayyit arba`a takbiraatin farda kifaayatin lillaahi ta`aala

نَوَيْتُ أَنْ أُصَلِّيَ صَلَاةَ الْجَنَازَةِ عَلَى الْمَيِّتِ أَرْبَعَ
تَكْبِيْرَاتٍ فَرْضَ كِفَايَةٍ لِلّٰهِ تَعَالَى

I intend to pray the Janazah prayer for the deceased as a communal obligation for the sake of Allah.

The Thana' (Praise of Allah)

Subhaana-kallaa-humma wabi hamdika wa tabaara-kasmuka wa ta`aala jadduka wa jalla thanaa'uka wa laa ilaaha ghayruk

سُبْحَانَكَ اللّٰهُمَّ وَبِحَمْدِكَ وَتَبَارَكَ اسْمُكَ وَتَعَالَى
جَدُّكَ وَجَلَّ ثَنَاؤُكَ وَلَا إِلٰهَ غَيْرُكَ

Glory be to You, O Allah, and all praises are due unto You. Blessed is Your name; high is Your majesty and great is Your praise. None is worthy of worship but You.

The Du`a if the Deceased is an Adult

Allaah hummaghfir li-hayyinaa wa mayyitinaa wa shaahidinaa wa ghaa'ibinaa wa saghirinaa wa kabirinaa wa dhakarinaa wa unthaanaa.

Allaahumma man ahyaytahu minnaa fa-ahyihi 'alal-Islam wa man tawaffaytahu minnaa fa-tawaffahu 'alal-Imaan.

اَللّٰهُمَّ اغْفِرْ لِحَيِّنَا وَمَيِّتِنَا وَشَاهِدِنَا وَغَائِبِنَا وَصَغِيرِنَا وَكَبِيرِنَا وَذَكَرِنَا وَأُنْثَانَا. اَللّٰهُمَّ مَنْ أَحْيَيْتَهُ مِنَّا فَأَحْيِهِ عَلَى الْإِسْلَامِ وَمَنْ تَوَفَّيْتَهُ مِنَّا فَتَوَفَّهُ عَلَى الْإِيمَانِ

O Allah! Forgive our living and our dead, and those who are present and to those who are absent, and to our young and our old, and to our males and females. O Allah! Whomever you grant to live from among us help him to live in Islam, and whomever you cause to die help him to die in Iman.

The Du`a if the Deceased is a Male Child

Allaahum maj`alhu lanaa faratan. Waj`alhu lanaa ajraw-wa zukhran. Waj`alhu lanaa shaafi`an wa mushaffa`a.

اَللَّهُمَّ اجْعَلْهُ لَنَا فَرَطًا وَاجْعَلْهُ لَنَا أَجْرًا وَّذُخْرًا
وَاجْعَلْهُ لَنَا شَافِعًا وَمُشَفَّعًا

O Allah! Make him a means of success for us; make him a means of reward and recompense for us and make him an intercessor for us whose intercession is granted by You.

The Du`a if the Deceased is a Female Child

Allaahum maj`alhaa lanaa faratan. Waj`alhaa lanaa ajraw-wa zukhran. Waj`alhaa lanaa shaafi`atan wa mushaffa`ah.

اَللّٰهُمَّ اجْعَلْهَا لَنَا فَرَطًا وَاجْعَلْهَا لَنَا أَجْرًا وَّذُخْرًا
وَاجْعَلْهَا لَنَا شَافِعَةً وَمُشَفَّعَةً

O Allah! Make her a means of success for us; make her a means of reward and recompense for us and make her an intercessor for us whose intercession is granted by You.

Lesson 13

Helping Others (Part Two)

We have discussed the importance of helping others. Helping others is one of the greatest acts of worship and the best way to get close to Allah. There are many ways in which we can be helpful to others. Let us read on further.

Giving Charity

Donating money is one way to help people. Islam encourages people to donate money to help the poor and needy. Allah tells us in the Qur'an that righteousness is not in doing religious actions, but righteousness is that we believe in Allah, the Last Day and spend money on our family, the orphans, the needy and the beggars (al-Baqara 2:177).

Some people may think that the best type of charity is to spend money on building mosques.

But many people do not realise that spending money on people, such as one's family, is also an important type of charity. Using our money to help improve the life of others, such as sponsoring someone's education or helping a poor person to get married, is one of the great forms of charity.

An important point about giving charity is that it should be done only for the pleasure of Allah. We should always expect the reward of that charity to come from Allah and not from the person who we helped. If a person gives charity just to show off, then that charity will lead the person to the Hellfire.

Whatever good action you do, it should be done with honesty, for the right reasons and not for getting something back in return. After giving charity, you should not hurt the feelings of the person by making fun of them or reminding them of the favour that you have done. This is a very bad thing to do and Allah forbids us from doing this (al-Baqara 2:262-264).

Feeding Others

Feeding people even if they are not poor is a great deed in Islam. However, feeding the poor and needy is far more important. Someone asked Prophet Muhammad ﷺ, "Which is the best deed in Islam?" The Prophet ﷺ replied, "Feed people and spread peace to people whether you know them or not." (al-Bukhari)

Feeding people and spreading peace are among the greatest deeds a Muslim can do. When Prophet Muhammad ﷺ entered Madinah after his emigration, the first thing that he commanded was to spread peace and to feed people (at-Tirmidhi). Even though the Prophet ﷺ was forced to leave his homeland, he did not tell people to be angry and fight. Instead he told people to spread peace and to help others.

The act of feeding the poor is very important. Today, in our country, there are children who are going to school hungry. Some parents need to go to food banks to get food for their children. We need to think about others and take care of one another. We should share our food with our friends and be concerned for them if they do not have food. There are needy people all around the world. Helping them is such an important deed that if we ignore it, it is described in the Qur'an as rejecting Islam.

Allah says that the people who push away the orphans and who do not feed the poor are denying the Din (i.e. Islam) (al-Ma`un 107:1-3). This means that those people who do not take care of the orphans and the poor people are among the people who do not follow Islam, even if they pray all the time.

Allah describes the disbelievers as those people who do not share their wealth with others. In the Qur'an, Allah says that when the disbelievers are told to spend their money to feed others, they reply, *"Should we feed the poor when Allah could have fed them?"* (Ya-Sin 36:47) This shows us the way the disbelievers think about the poor people and their bad attitude towards them. A true Muslim does not think like this; Muslims care about others. A true Muslim always shares his or her wealth and belongings to help people who do not have as much as they do.

Visiting the Sick and Bereaved People

Just like feeding the poor, visiting someone when they are sick is also a very important deed in Islam. These days very few people go to visit others when they are sick. Most people are too busy, or they think that the person will become better after a few days, so they do not bother going to visit them. They might just phone and ask about how they are doing.

Prophet Muhammad ﷺ taught us the importance of visiting the sick. He said that on the Day of Judgement, Allah will say to a person, "Son of Adam, I was sick, but you did not visit Me."

The person will reply, "My Lord, how could I visit You when You are the Lord of the Worlds?"

Allah will say, "Did you not know that one of My servants was sick and you didn't visit him? If you had visited him, you would have found Me there."

Then Allah will say, "Son of Adam, I needed food, but you did not feed Me."

The person will reply, "My Lord, how could I feed You when You are the Lord of the Worlds?"

Allah will say, "Did you not know that one of My servants was hungry, but you did not feed him? If you had fed him, you would have found its reward with Me."

Then Allah will say, "Son of Adam, I was thirsty, but you did not give Me something to drink."

The person will reply, "My Lord, how could I give You something to drink when You are the Lord of the Worlds?"

Allah will say, "Did you not know that one of My servants was thirsty, but you did not give him something to drink? If you had given him something to drink, you would have found its reward with Me." (al-Bukhari)

Lesson 14

Sirah: The Migration (Hijrah)

The Prophet ﷺ spent his days and nights telling people about Allah and calling them to Islam. After his uncle Abu Talib passed away, the non-Muslims in Makkah started to treat the Prophet ﷺ worse than before. They did their best to fight against Islam. Only a small number of people in Makkah became Muslims and believed in Allah and His Prophet ﷺ. However, this did not stop the Prophet ﷺ in telling people about Allah's message. He never lost hope and he continued in his mission and worked hard to call his people to Allah.

The Delegation from Yathrib

During the month of Dhu al-Hijjah, Arabs belonging to different tribes and families would come from all parts of Arabia to visit the

Ka`bah. During this month, the Prophet ﷺ used to spread the message of Islam to the other Arabian tribes. He would visit each tribe one by one and tell them to worship only Allah and to not worship idols. He would tell them to believe in his prophethood and to accept him as Allah's Messenger.

One of the tribes that the Prophet ﷺ visited was the Khazraj tribe from Yathrib (Madinah). The Khazraj were Arabs and they were idol worshippers. They were at war with the Jews that lived in Yathrib. The Jews would always remind them that the time of the final Prophet was coming closer and that they would follow him when he came, and they would kill the Arabs. So, when Prophet Muhammad ﷺ spoke to them they were interested in what he had to say because they wanted to know if he was the same prophet that the Jews told them about.

There were six men from the Khazraj tribe. When they met the Prophet ﷺ they listened to what he told them, and they accepted his message. They believed in him as Allah's Messenger, so they accepted Islam and became Muslims. They asked the Prophet ﷺ to give them time to speak to the other people from their tribe in Yathrib.

There were two main Arab tribes in Yathrib, the Aws and the Khazraj. These two tribes hated each other, and they always fought against each other. The Khazraj tribesmen hoped that through Islam they could unite the two Arab tribes and bring an end to their wars. So, the Prophet ﷺ accepted their request.

The Khazraj tribesmen returned to Yathrib (Madinah) and called their people to Islam. They spread its message among the people of Yathrib and there was not a single house left in Yathrib that did not know about the Prophet ﷺ.

The Pledge of al-`Aqabah

The following year, the Khazraj tribesmen returned to Makkah. This time, there were twelve of them and they met the Prophet ﷺ at a place called al-`Aqabah. These twelve people were from both the Aws and the Khazraj tribes and they gave the Prophet ﷺ their pledge of allegiance. The pledge of allegiance was a promise that they made to the Prophet ﷺ to fully follow and support him. This pledge of allegiance came to be known as the first pledge of al-`Aqabah.

The twelve people from Yathrib promised the Prophet ﷺ that they would not worship idols, steal, be rude and impolite, kill their children, tell lies about others or disobey the Prophet ﷺ.

The Prophet ﷺ sent his Companion Mus`ab bin `Umayr to Yathrib to teach them more about Islam. Mus`ab bin `Umayr used to lead the prayers to keep the peace between the Aws and Khazraj tribes.

In the following year, which was the thirteenth year of Prophethood, 73 men and 2 women came from Yathrib to meet the Prophet ﷺ. They also pledged their allegiance to him and invited him and the Muslims of Makkah to emigrate to Yathrib (Madinah). They promised to support the Prophet ﷺ and to protect him even if they had to give their lives.

The Prophet ﷺ accepted their request and he commanded the Muslims of Makkah to leave their homes and to emigrate to Yathrib because it was safer for them.

The Quraysh Plans

One by one the Muslims left Makkah until none of them were left except for Abu Bakr as-Siddiq, `Ali bin Abi Talib and those Muslims who could not leave because they were kept behind by their non-Muslim families. Prophet Muhammad ﷺ also remained behind in Makkah and waited until Allah commanded him to leave.

During this time, the Quraysh noticed that many of the Muslims had left Makkah. They knew that the Muslims had found a new homeland and that this would give them protection. They wanted to destroy Islam and so they came up with a plan to kill the Prophet ﷺ.

The Quraysh leaders gathered at a place called Dar an-Nadwa, to discuss what action they should take. In this meeting, Iblis (Shaytan) also came. He made himself look like a Shaykh (a wise old man) from Najd, which is a place east of Makkah and Madinah. Iblis listened to everyone's ideas and he did not like any of them until he heard Abu Jahl's idea.

Abu Jahl suggested that a strong young man should be chosen from every tribe of the Quraysh to attack Prophet Muhammad ﷺ at the same time. In this way instead of one tribe getting blamed, the blame of the attack would be equally spread out between the different tribes and this would force the Banu Hashim (the Prophet's clan) to accept blood money and it would make it difficult for them to take revenge.

When the Najdi (Shaytan) heard this suggestion, he was pleased with it. He said that it was the best suggestion. So, everyone in the meeting agreed to this idea and they went to put the plan into action.

Allah Protects His Prophet

Angel Jibra'il told the Prophet ﷺ what the Quraysh were planning to do. So, the Prophet ﷺ told his younger cousin `Ali to sleep in his bed. He told `Ali to stay behind in Makkah and to give back the valuables that the Prophet ﷺ was keeping safe for people.

The non-believers, many who hated Islam and did not believe in the Prophet ﷺ, would still trust the Prophet ﷺ with their valuables, because they knew that no one was more trustworthy and truthful than him. So `Ali remained behind in Makkah for another three days to return these valuables to their owners, and to fulfil the Prophet's trust.

On the night of the Prophet's migration, while `Ali was sleeping in the Prophet's bed, the young men that were chosen by the Quraysh were outside the Prophet's house waiting to put their evil plan into action. As the Prophet ﷺ was leaving the house, he took a handful of dust and recited the first nine verses of Surah Yasin. He then threw the dust in the direction of the young men and they all became temporarily blind. The Prophet ﷺ walked past them all and safely made his way to the house of Abu Bakr as-Siddiq without being seen by any of them.

When the men broke into the house to attack the Prophet ﷺ they found `Ali in the bed instead and they realised that they had been tricked.

The Companion of the Cave

When the Prophet ﷺ met Abu Bakr as-Siddiq, he told him that Allah had given him permission to emigrate to Madinah. When Abu Bakr as-Siddiq found out that he was going to go together with the Prophet ﷺ on the journey, he was so happy that he cried tears of joy.

Before, he had asked the Prophet ﷺ for permission to leave for Yathrib (Madinah), but the Prophet ﷺ told him to not rush because Allah had chosen a travelling companion for him. Abu Bakr as-Siddiq guessed that his travelling companion was the Prophet ﷺ so he prepared two riding camels for the journey, and so when it was confirmed that he was travelling with the Prophet ﷺ, he was full of happiness and joy.

The Prophet ﷺ and Abu Bakr as-Siddiq set off on their journey to Yathrib (Madinah). Even though Madinah was in the north of Makkah, they went in the southern direction to take shelter in the Cave Thawr. The Quraysh soon realised that the Prophet ﷺ had left Makkah, so they made an announcement, telling everyone that whoever captures the Prophet ﷺ would receive 100 camels as a prize.

This was a great reward that made many horsemen from every direction of Makkah go out to find the Prophet ﷺ. The Prophet ﷺ and Abu Bakr as-Siddiq remained in Cave Thawr for three days. While they stayed in the cave, Abu Bakr's elder daughter Asma' would bring them food in the evening and his son `Abd Allah would look after their camels and bring them news of what was happening in Makkah.

During this time, some of the non-believers came near the cave looking for the Prophet ﷺ. Seeing them so close, Abu Bakr as-Siddiq was worried for the Prophet's safety. "If they look down a little, they will see us." He said. But the Prophet ﷺ reassured him saying, "Do not worry. Allah is with us."

The non-believers came to the entrance of the cave. They saw that it was covered by a spider's web and a bird's nest was next to it. When they saw this, they thought that nobody was in the cave because the spider's web had not been broken and the birds would not have made their nest in a disturbed place. So they returned without realising that the Prophet ﷺ and Abu Bakr as-Siddiq were hiding there. This was a miracle from Allah to protect his beloved Prophet ﷺ.

Arrival in Quba

After three days had passed, the Prophet ﷺ and Abu Bakr as-Siddiq left Cave Thawr. They continued on their way to Yathrib (Madinah). The journey was a long and dangerous one. After two weeks, they reached a place called Quba which was a few miles from Madinah, on Monday the 12th of Rabi al-`Awwal (27th September). The Prophet ﷺ stayed in Quba. During his stay, the Prophet ﷺ made the first mosque. He stayed in Quba for several days and he led the first Jumu`a prayer there. After this the Prophet ﷺ continued the journey to Madinah.

The migration (journey) to Madinah was a key turning point in the history of Islam. The Muslim calendar (Hijri calendar) starts with the migration to Madinah. The migration and the first year of the Hijri Calendar took place in the year 622 CE and today more than have 1400 years have passed since this important event took place.

Lesson 15

Belief in the Unseen

Over the past centuries, humankind has made great advancements in knowledge. Through modern technology, we have learnt many new things that were unknown to us before the modern era. We thought that everything we could see, hear or touch was all that existed in this world. But we soon came to realise how limited our knowledge was.

We learnt that there was a whole new world at the microscopic level, which contained tiny things that could not be seen with our eyes alone. We also learnt that the universe was so large that it is not possible for us to imagine how big it is. Even more surprising was that we came to learn that everything that we can see, hear or touch is only a very small part of the world around us and that most of physical reality is hidden from our senses.

All of this shows us that human beings have a small amount of knowledge and that they do not know much. In the Qur'an, Allah tells us that human beings were given only a little knowledge (al-Isra' 17:85). If we understand this, then it means that we need to be humble and recognise that we do not know everything. It means that we should be open minded and realise that the world around us is not everything that we see, hear or touch, but there are many things that we cannot observe with our senses.

The part of the world that we can see with our eyes, hear with our ears and touch with our hand is called **`Alam ash-Shahadah** (the visible world). Whereas the part of the world that we cannot see with our eyes, hear with our ears and touch with our hand is called **`Alam al-Ghayb** (the invisible world). Allah has given us access to the visible world, but He has not given us access to the invisible world.

How Can We Learn About the Invisible World?

Allah has hidden the invisible world from us as a test of our faith. It will become visible to us when we die and enter the life hereafter. However, in this life, Allah informed Prophet Muhammad ﷺ about the invisible world, and this is how we know about it. It is only through the means of **revelation** that we know what exists in the unseen realm.

When Allah informed Prophet Muhammad ﷺ about the invisible world, the Prophet ﷺ received its knowledge. Through his hadith, he taught the Companions about the **unseen realities (ghayb)**, and so this knowledge was passed onto them. The Companions then passed this knowledge to their students, until it reached us today from one generation to the next. This is how we come to know about the invisible world.

As Muslims, we must believe in whatever knowledge Prophet Muhammad ﷺ has given to us regarding the unseen matters. We must accept them wholeheartedly and recognise that it is part of our religion. It does not matter if we cannot understand them, because these matters are outside of our normal understanding. As mentioned earlier, we have only a small amount of knowledge; we should realise our limitations and submit to the authority of the Prophets, because they were the ones who were given this special knowledge.

Some of the unseen realities belonging to the invisible world (`Alam al-Ghayb) that we must believe in are mentioned below.

Angels (Mala'ika)

We must believe in the existence of angels. Allah created angels from light and they can take any shape or form, including human beings. Angels are Allah's servants and they cannot disobey Allah. They do whatever Allah orders them to do. They do not eat, drink or get married, and they cannot be described as male or female. Allah created them with wings.

Allah has assigned the angels many duties. Some of the famous angels and their duties are detailed as follows.

1. ANGEL JIBRA'IL: He carries Allah's message to the Prophets.

2. ANGEL MIKA'IL: He commands the rain and wind.

3. ANGEL IZRA'IL: He is the angel of death (Malak al-Mawt).

4. ANGEL ISRAFIL: He will blow the trumpet on the Day of Judgement.

5. ANGELS RAQIB and `ATID: These two angels are known as the 'Honourable Scribes' (Kiraman Katibin) and they keep a record of all our deeds. Raqib is the angel on the right shoulder who records our good deeds and `Atid is the

angel on the left shoulder who records our bad deeds.

6. ANGELS MUNKAR and NAKIR: These two angels question the dead person in the grave.

7. ANGEL RIDWAN: The guardian who oversees Paradise (Jannah).

8. ANGEL MALIK: The guardian who oversees the Hellfire (Jahannum).

9. THE MU`AQQABAT: These are the ten angels who take care of every person until their time of death arrives.

10. THE HAMLAT AL-`ARSH: These are the eight angels who carry Allah's throne.

Jinn

We must believe in the existence of the Jinn. Allah created the Jinn from smokeless fire. Like the angels, they can take different shapes and forms, but they are not like angels, because they eat, drink and get married. Among the Jinn are those that are believers and are worshipful servants of Allah, and there are those that are disbelievers and disobedient to Allah. The Jinn live separate from human beings in places far away from human civilisation; they can see us, but we cannot see them.

Paradise (Jannah) and Hell (Jahannum)

We must believe in the existence of Paradise and Hell. Allah created them both and only He knows their true location. They will never come to an end as Allah has commanded that they will remain forever. Paradise and Hell are humanity's final destination, and after the Day of Judgement we will live within them forever.

In Paradise, there are no religious duties or obligations. It is a place of reward and enjoyment.

The people of Paradise will never suffer any hardship or difficulty, and Allah will never be angry or displeased with them. They will only be inclined towards goodness, and they will never do anything that is displeasing to Allah. Allah will always be happy with the people of Paradise, and He will speak to them and they will see Him, like the way they see the full moon shining bright in the night sky.

Hell, on the other hand, is a place of Allah's punishment. There are strict angels there who do not disobey Allah, and they punish the evildoers. The people of the Hellfire will want the punishment to stop, but it will not be stopped. Some will remain there forever. Allah will not talk to them, and they will be left out from His company and nearness.

The Soul (Ruh)

The soul is a secret of Allah. No one knows its reality except for Him. The soul was created before our bodies, and it is breathed into our bodies by an angel. Even when we die, our soul will continue to exist without our bodies because the soul does not die. Before we were born into this world, Allah questioned our souls asking them if He was their Lord and all the souls said, "Yes."

The Throne (`Arsh and Kursi)

The `Arsh and Kursi are the throne of Allah. They are both gigantic heavenly figures made of light. The Kursi is attached below the `Arsh and is much smaller than the `Arsh. However, the Kursi contains all the seven heavens.

Compared to the Kursi, this whole universe is like the size of a pea in the middle of a football pitch, and the size of the Kursi compared to the `Arsh is also the same. No one knows their reality except for Allah. Our minds cannot imagine Allah's throne; it is not like anything we know. Allah created them but does not need them. They are signs of His greatness, authority and might.

The Tablet (Lawh) and the Pen (Qalam)

The Lawh and the Qalam are both large heavenly figures made from light. Only Allah knows their reality and they are nothing like what we see or know. We only know them by their name and purpose, and they are not like anything that comes to our mind or imagination. Allah commanded the Qalam (Pen) to write everything that was, is and will be until the Day of Judgement, and the destiny of every person is recorded on the Lawh (Tablet).

All these hidden realities are from the secrets of Allah. We should not think deeply about them because they are outside the understanding of our minds. We accept whatever Prophet Muhammad ﷺ told us about them, because the knowledge of these unseen matters was gifted to him by His Creator.

Lesson 16

Sirah: Arrival to the City of Light

As the arrival of the Prophet ﷺ came closer, the people of Yathrib were overjoyed and very excited. They would come out into the desert every morning because they wanted to be the first to greet the Prophet ﷺ when he arrived. They would remain out in the desert all day until they could find no shade to protect them from the blazing heat of the sun.

On the day of the Prophet's arrival, they remained sitting outside just as they had been doing the days before and when there was no shade left to protect them from the sun, they returned home. As they were entering their homes, they heard a voice telling them that the Prophet of Allah had entered Yathrib, so they hurried back outside to greet the Prophet ﷺ.

The people of Yathrib came out together to greet the Prophet ﷺ as he entered the small desert town. Most of them had not seen the Prophet ﷺ before and they could not tell which of the two camel riders he was. So, Abu Bakr as-Siddiq stood up on his camel and used his cloak to shade the Prophet ﷺ from the heat. In this way, the people were able to recognise the Prophet ﷺ. They were overjoyed with happiness. In their excitement and delight, the people of Yathrib (Madinah) sang the following song to welcome the Prophet ﷺ:

طَلَعَ الْبَدْرُ عَلَيْنَا مِنْ ثَنِيَّاتِ الْوَدَاعِ

وَجَبَ الشُّكْرُ عَلَيْنَا مَا دَعَا لِلَّهِ دَاعٍ

أَيُّهَا الْمَبْعُوثُ فِينَا جِئْتَ بِالْأَمْرِ الْمُطَاعِ

جِئْتَ شَرَّفْتَ الْمَدِينَةَ مَرْحَباً يَا خَيْرَ دَاعٍ

O the white moon rose over us,
from the valley of Wada`
And we owe it to show gratefulness,
where the call is to Allah.

O you who were raised among us,
coming with the word to be obeyed.

You have brought to this city nobleness,
welcome best caller to God's way.

Building the Prophet's Mosque

All the men, women and children of Madinah were celebrating the arrival of the Prophet ﷺ. The different tribes in Madinah all wanted the Prophet ﷺ to live with them. The Prophet ﷺ did not say no to any of his Companions. Instead, he told them to untie his camel and to let it walk because the camel was ordered by Allah to sit in the place where the Prophet's mosque and house would be built.

The camel made its way to Yathrib (Madinah) where it entered the neighbourhood of the Banu Najjar, in an open field outside of the house of **Abu Ayyub al-Ansari.** It sat in this empty field where the Prophet's mosque is today. Here the Prophet ﷺ and his Companions worked together to build **Masjid an-Nabawi (the Prophet's mosque)**, which is still visited by millions of Muslims every year. The Prophet ﷺ worked alongside his Companions when building the mosque, to teach the Muslims the importance of working with one's own hands.

The small town of Yathrib was renamed **Madinah an-Nabi (the City of the Prophet** ﷺ**)**. Madinah was the Prophet's new home and it was the Prophet's final resting place. While the Prophet's mosque was being built, the Prophet ﷺ stayed with his Companion Abu Ayyub al-Ansari.

The young girls from Banu Najjar were full of joy and happiness. They sang songs praising the Prophet ﷺ, beating their Daff (tambourine) and saying:

نَحْنُ جَوَارٍ مِنْ بَنِي النَّجَّارْ

يَا حَبَّذَا مُحَمَّدٌ مِنْ جَارْ

We are girls from the children of Najjar
What an excellent neighbour is Muhammad

When the Prophet ﷺ heard the song, he said, "Allah knows that you are dear to me." (Ibn Majah)

The Message of Peace

During the Prophet's ﷺ first days in Madinah he gave his first talk to the Muslims. He told them to worship Allah and to protect themselves from the Hellfire, by giving even half a date in charity.

Even though the Prophet ﷺ was treated very badly by the people in Makkah and was forced to leave his home, he did not complain about the way the Quraysh treated him. He only talked about being thankful to Allah and about following His commandments. He continued to teach his followers to be peaceful and kind and helpful to others.

`Abd Allah bin Salam, who was a Jewish Rabbi, mentions that when the Prophet ﷺ entered Madinah, the people were delighted, and they rushed to meet him. So he also went to see the Prophet ﷺ. `Abd Allah bin Salam said, "When I saw the face of the Prophet ﷺ, the first thing that he said was: 'O people! Spread peace, feed others and pray while the people are sleeping; you will enter Paradise in peace.'" (at-Tirmidhi)

The Prophet ﷺ was the new leader of Madinah and he wanted to bring together the different tribes. Every country has a constitution which tells people how a country works and what rules to follow. The Prophet ﷺ made the first constitution in history called the '**Constitution of Madinah**'. In this constitution, the Prophet ﷺ united the Muslim and Jewish tribes and made them into one community (Ummah).

He also made a pact of brotherhood between the emigrants from Makkah, who were known as the **Muhajirin**, and the helpers from Madinah, who were known as the **Ansar**. The Muhajirin (Immigrants) and the Ansar (Helpers) were the two main groups of Muslims who were living in Madinah.

In the pact of brotherhood, Prophet Muhammad ﷺ took one person from the Muhajirin (Immigrants) and one person from the Ansar and made them brothers. The Prophet ﷺ took his younger cousin `Ali as his brother. The Prophet ﷺ did not want to divide the Aws and Khazraj and so chose someone from his own family. The Prophet's choice also shows the great status of `Ali that he was taken as the Prophet's brother. Only a person close to the Prophet ﷺ could have enjoyed such a status.

The Ansar helped their brothers from the Muhajirin and shared their wealth with them so

that the new immigrants (the Muhajirin) were able to start their lives in Madinah and become useful members of society.

The Introduction of the Adhan

When the Prophet's mosque was built, the Muslims needed to find a way to call people to the mosque when it was time to pray. There was a suggestion to raise a flag, or to use a horn or a drum like the Christians and the Jews, but the Prophet ﷺ did not like any of these suggestions.

So, the Muslims went away to think about this matter. During this time, one of the Companions saw a dream in which the Adhan was being recited. The Prophet ﷺ was told about the dream and from then on, the Adhan became the symbol of Islam because it was a good way of calling people to prayer and the Companion **Bilal bin Rabah** was the first Muezzin.

After the migration to Madinah, new Islamic rules were revealed by Allah. Islam was becoming strongly recognised in the newly founded city of Madinah. The Salah was performed five times a day in congregation in the Prophet's mosque. Fasting in the month of Ramadan became obligatory and the amount of money to be given as Zakah and Sadaqat al-Fitr was made clear. The first `Id prayer was also performed in the second year after Hijrah.

Changing the Direction of the Qiblah

During the month of Rajab, 17 months after the Hijrah, the direction of the Qiblah changed from Masjid al-Aqsa, in Jerusalem, to the Ka`bah, in Makkah. Allah gave the command to change the direction of the Qiblah while the Prophet ﷺ was leading his Companions in the prayer. As the Prophet ﷺ was leading the prayer, he moved from his place, which was facing the northern side of the mosque, and moved to the back of the congregation facing the southern side.

When the Companions saw that the Prophet ﷺ had changed his direction, they were not sure what to do. They were not sure whether they should continue facing Masjid al-Aqsa, or whether they should change their direction as well to face the Ka`bah. This was a great test for the Companions. Do they follow their own understanding of Islam and continue with what they already know, or do they follow the Prophet ﷺ?

The Companions, who belong to the greatest group of Muslims, knew that obedience to the Prophet ﷺ is the true Islam. They knew that they could not worship Allah properly if they were not obedient to Prophet Muhammad ﷺ and if they did not follow him in everything that he did. So, the Companions, in their love and commitment to the Prophet ﷺ, turned around and faced the new Qiblah, facing the southern direction of the Ka`bah. They did not think twice about following and obeying Prophet Muhammad ﷺ.

Lesson 17

The Congregational Prayer

One of the great symbols of Islam is the 'Congregational Prayer' (Salat al-Jama`ah). Praying in congregation means that we perform the Salah together.

As Muslims, we are brothers and sisters to one another. We belong to one Ummah, a community of believers. Praying together in congregation is an important way of bringing our Muslim community together. Prophet Muhammad ﷺ commanded us to perform the prayer in congregation because it is 27 times better than when you pray alone (al-Bukhari).

The Benefits of Praying in Congregation

There are many good things about praying in congregation. Some of them are:

1. Praying together helps to build a strong and healthy community. It teaches us that we should work together in doing good actions.

2. By praying together, we can look after other people in our community and share in each other's happiness and sadness. If someone is ill or is having a hard time, we can find out about it and go to visit them.

3. Praying together creates discipline and respect for each other. It teaches us to be united and to work together under a single leadership.

4. Praying in congregation teaches us to be on time and to be organised in our life.

5. Praying in congregation teaches us that everybody is equal and should be treated the same as each other. It stops people from thinking that they are better than others.

How to Offer the Salat al-Jama`ah

The Congregational Prayer (Salat al-Jama`ah) is performed in a similar way to when praying alone, but there are some important differences. Here is a step-by-step guide to performing the two unit prayer in congregation.

1. Start by reciting the intention for the prayer. In this intention, you must say that you are going to perform the prayer behind the Imam.

2. When the Imam makes the Takbir at-Tahrimah, say the takbir quietly. In the congregational prayer you must follow the Imam and not perform any action before him.

3. Recite the Thana' (Praise of Allah) quietly and then remain silent.

4. The Imam will recite the Ta`awwudh (Seeking Refuge in Allah) and Tasmiyah (In the Name of Allah) silently on your behalf.

5. Then the Imam will recite Surat al-Fatihah. If it is the Fajr, Maghrib and `Isha' prayers, the Imam will recite it out aloud. But if it is the Zuhr and `Asr prayers, the Imam will recite it quietly

to himself. Do not recite anything; just remain silent and listen to the Imam's recitation.

6. In the Fajr, Maghrib and `Isha' prayers, when the Imam completes reciting Surat al-Fatihah loudly, say 'Amin' quietly. Some people say it loudly, which is fine because Muslims can pray differently.

7. Then the Imam will recite the Qur'an. Listen to the Imam's recitation and do not say anything.

8. Then the Imam will go into the Ruku` (Bowing Position). He will say the takbir loudly. Say the takbir quietly to yourself and follow the Imam. During the Ruku` (Bowing Position), recite 'Subhaana Rabbi al-`Azeem' quietly.

9. Then the Imam will move into the Qawmah (the Short Standing Position). He will say

'Sami'a Allaahu liman hamidah' loudly. Follow the Imam into this position and say 'Rabbanaa lakal hamd' quietly.

10. Then follow the Imam into the Sajdah (Prostration Position). Perform the two prostrations (Sajdah) with the Imam and recite 'Subhaana Rabbi al-A`laa' quietly.

This completes the first unit (rak`ah). Follow the Imam into the next unit (rak`ah) by following steps 5 to 10. Then complete the prayer by following the next two steps.

11. At the end of the prayer, the Imam will sit down for the Qa`dah (the Sitting Position). During this position, recite the Tashahhud (the Bearing Testimony), Salat Ibrahimiyya (Abrahamic Salutation) and then a Du`a (Supplication) quietly to yourself.

12. After this the Imam will perform the Salam (The Ending Position). The Imam will say the Salam loudly. Follow the Imam as he turns his face right and then left and say the Salam quietly.

In the three or four unit prayer, only recite Tashahhud (the Bearing Testimony) silently to yourself in the first sitting (step 11). After some time, the Imam will say the takbir and stand up for the third unit. Say the takbir quietly and follow the Imam.

In the third and fourth units during the Qiyam (Standing Position), the Imam will only recite Surat al-Fatihah quietly to himself. Remain silent during this time. Follow the Imam into the Ruku` (Bowing Position) and carry out steps 8 to 10.

In the final unit, after performing the two Prostrations, follow steps 11 and 12 to complete the prayer.

If You Are Late to the Prayer

You can join the congregational prayer at any time. Here are some rules:

- If you have missed a unit (rak`ah), you should make up that unit (rak`ah) at the end of the prayer.

- When the Imam makes the Salam (the Ending Position), you do not make the Salam with the Imam. After the Imam makes the first Salam, you stand up and make up the units that you have missed.

- When we join the prayer late, we continue from the same unit as the Imam. So, if the Imam is in the second unit, you start your prayer from the second unit and you make up the first unit after the Imam's prayer.

- If you join the prayer before the Imam gets up from the Ruku` (Bowing Position), you have got there in time to read that unit (rak`ah) and you do not need to make it up. If you join as the

Imam is getting up, you will need to make up the unit (rak`ah) at the end of the prayer.

- When you start the prayer, if the Imam is in the Ruku` (Bowing Position), you need to perform the Takbir at-Tahrimah in the standing position before going into the Ruku` (Bowing Position).

Lesson 18

Prophet Sulayman عليه السلام

When Prophet Dawud عليه السلام passed away, his son Prophet Sulayman عليه السلام became the king. Prophet Sulayman عليه السلام inherited his father's kingdom, prophethood and wisdom, and he was one of Allah's greatest Prophets.

Allah had blessed Prophet Sulayman عليه السلام with wisdom and understanding at a young age. He showed his wisdom when two women came to him fighting over a baby. They had left their babies together in one place, but a wolf had come and taken one of them. Both women wanted that baby and said that it belonged to them. So, they asked Prophet Sulayman عليه السلام to decide who the real mother of the baby was.

Prophet Sulayman عليه السلام listened to their story and then asked for a knife to be brought to him. He then ordered for the baby to be cut in half, and for one half to be given to both women. When the mother of the baby heard this, she cried. "No! Give it to her; it is her son." Seeing that the woman did not want the baby to be harmed, Prophet Sulayman ﷺ knew that she was its real mother, and so he ordered the baby to be given to her.

Prophet Sulayman ﷺ grew up to become a kind and fair king. He prayed to Allah to grant him a kingdom the likes of which nobody after him could ever have. Allah accepted his prayer and gave him the power to control the winds and to understand the language of the birds and animals. No one before him had ever spoken to the animals and understood what they said. He also had control over the Jinn, and they would dive into the deep ocean and bring back pearls.

The Jinn would follow every command given to them, and they could not disobey him.

One day, Prophet Sulayman عليه السلام was marching with his army, which was made up of men, Jinn and birds. They reached a field of ants. One of the ants hearing the footsteps in the distance said to the others, "O ants, enter your homes, so that Sulayman and his army do not crush you without realising." When Prophet Sulayman عليه السلام heard what the ant said, he smiled. He thanked Allah for this blessing. He then ordered his army to avoid the field where the ants were and to follow a separate path.

One day while Prophet Sulayman عليه السلام was checking his troops he found that Hud Hud, the Hoopoe bird, was missing.

"Where is Hud Hud? I do not see him," said Prophet Sulayman ﵇, "I will certainly punish him for being absent, unless he brings me a good excuse."

As soon as Prophet Sulayman ﵇ said this, Hud Hud appeared. He brought news about the people of Saba, who lived in Yemen. He told Prophet Sulayman ﵇ about Queen Bilqis and her mighty kingdom. He found them worshipping the sun besides Allah.

When Prophet Sulayman ﵇ learned about this, he decided to write a letter to Queen Bilqis and invite her to the worship of the one true God, Allah. He gave Hud Hud this letter and ordered him to deliver it to her.

When Hud Hud dropped the letter to Queen Bilqis, she opened it and saw the words written by Prophet Sulayman عليه السلام. After starting with the name of Allah, he commanded her to submit before Allah, and to accept the worship of the One God, Allah, and not to resist.

Queen Bilqis gathered her commanders and asked them for their advice on what to do. "We are powerful and great warriors," they declared, "but the command is yours. So, you should decide what to do."

Queen Bilqis did not like the idea of war. "No doubt when kings enter a town, they destroy it and dishonour its people," she said, "and they will do the same." Instead, she decided to send Prophet

Sulayman ﷺ gifts and waited to see his reply.

When those gifts arrived, Prophet Sulayman ﷺ got angry. He did not want gifts. He only wanted them to worship Allah. So, he returned their gifts and promised to send an army if they did not submit to Allah.

Queen Bilqis agreed to submit and she decided to go to Jerusalem and meet Prophet Sulayman ﷺ. Before she arrived at the palace, Prophet Sulayman ﷺ asked his courtiers who among them can bring her throne to him.

A powerful Jinn stood up and said, "I can bring it before you rise up from your seat." But a knowledgeable man stood up and said, "I can bring it to you before the twinkling of an eye." And before Prophet Sulayman ﷺ could say anything, the throne of Queen Bilqis was there before him. Prophet Sulayman ﷺ praised Allah and thanked Him for His blessings.

When Queen Bilqis arrived at the palace, she was shown her throne, but she did not recognise it at first. She then realised Allah's favours upon Prophet Sulayman ﷺ. She saw the wonders of his palace and went into one room where the floor was made out of crystal slabs under which water flowed. She lifted her skirt thinking it was flowing water, but when her feet did not get wet, she realised she was wrong and she submitted herself to Allah, the Lord of the Worlds.

Lesson 19

Sirah: The Battle of Badr

Ever since the Muhajirin (the Immigrants) settled in Madinah, the Quraysh were even more angry towards the Muslims. They could not rest in peace until they brought an end to Islam. They continued harming the Muslims who remained in Makkah. Many of them were locked up in chains and were not allowed to leave their homes.

The Quraysh treated the Muslims in a very harsh way, and for this reason, when the Muslims migrated to Madinah, Allah allowed them to fight back in self-defence. Before this the Muslims were not allowed to fight back even in self-defence. It was a test for them and they had to remain patient with the difficulties that they were facing, but now they could fight back to protect themselves.

Nearly a year after the Hijrah, Prophet Muhammad ﷺ sent out a group of soldiers to show the enemies of Islam that the Muslims were

strong, and to persuade the Quraysh to accept peace with them. But the Quraysh did not want peace. They saw the new city of Madinah as a threat to their business trade with Syria, because Madinah was on the way to Syria and they were afraid that their caravans could be attacked easily because they had to go past Madinah on their way to Syria.

Abu Sufyan's Caravan

The Quraysh had taken the wealth of the Muhajirin (Muslim immigrants) that they had left behind in Makkah when they had emigrated. The Quraysh were now carrying all that wealth to Syria to sell it in their trading trip.

In the month of Ramadan, the Prophet ﷺ received news that this caravan was now returning from Syria. It was being led by Abu Sufyan. So, the Prophet ﷺ gathered a group of over 300 people to stop the caravan and to take back what the Quraysh took from them.

Abu Sufyan found out that the Muslims were heading towards them. So, he sent a message to the Quraysh in Makkah and asked them to come and bring back up to protect his caravan. When the message reached the Quraysh, the leaders of the Quraysh prepared for war in excitement and they gathered an army of one thousand men to fight against the Muslims.

In the meantime, Abu Sufyan moved his caravan away from the direction of Madinah and travelled closer to the seashore hoping that the Muslim army would not reach him. When the trading caravan had gone past Madinah, Abu Sufyan was happy and relieved because the Muslim army would not be able to reach him and his caravan was safe.

But the Quraysh had already left Makkah and were approaching an area called Badr. Abu Sufyan sent a message to them to return home to Makkah, but Abu Jahl got angry and he refused to go back. He wanted to fight against the Muslims and to destroy them so that no Arab would ever stand up to the Quraysh again. So, the Quraysh continued with their march until they met the Muslim army at Badr.

The Wells of Badr

When the Prophet ﷺ received news that the Quraysh were still on their way and did not return to Makkah, he discussed what to do next with the Muhajirin (Immigrants) and the Ansar (Helpers).

Al-Miqdad bin `Amr from the Muhajirin (Emigrants), stood up and said, "O Messenger of

Allah, do what Allah has shown you because we are with you. By Allah, we will not say to you what the Bani Isra'il said to Prophet Musa ﷵ, that 'You along with your Lord go and fight; we are sitting right here.' Rather, we say, 'You along with your Lord go and fight; we are with you and we will fight.'"

Sa`d bin Mu`adh from the Ansar (Helpers), also said words of encouragement and said that they would fight alongside the Prophet ﷺ. Hearing the replies from both groups, the Prophet ﷺ was happy, and he ordered the Muslims to make their way to Badr.

On the night before the battle, Prophet Muhammad ﷺ spent the night worshipping Allah and asking Him for help. Allah promised him victory and sent angels to fight alongside the Muslims.

On the day of the battle, the angels came down. They wore white turbans and they fought together with the Muslims against the Quraysh. Afterwards some of the people who survived the Battle of Badr described how they saw the non-believers being being killed, even though they could see no one attacking them with a sword.

The Prophet ﷺ introduced a new way of fighting in Arabia. He ordered the Muslim soldiers to stand in rows like the rows of the Salah. He put the lancers (those who carry spears) in the first row for protection against the enemy horse riders and he put the archers in the second row to stop the enemy from coming forward. This style of fighting was strange for the Arabs and the Quraysh did not expect it because they were used to attacking without any planning, order or discipline.

Yawm al-Furqan (The Day of Differentiation)

When the two armies faced each other on the battlefield, it was the morning of Friday 17th Ramadan 2 AH (After Hijrah). `Utbah bin Rabi`ah, who was one of the leaders of the Quraysh, came forward with his brother Shaybah and his son Walid and challenged the Muslims to a swordfight. Three young men from the Ansar accepted the challenge and stood in front of them, but `Utbah said no to them and challenged the Muslims from the Muhajirin (Immigrants) instead. So, the Prophet ﷺ put forward three of his relatives, `Ubaydah bin Harith, Hamzah bin `Abd al-Muttalib and `Ali bin Abi Talib, to take part in the swordfight.

Straightaway Hamzah killed Shaybah and `Ali killed Walid. `Ubaydah bin Harith and `Utbah both hit each other, but eventually `Utbah was killed by Hamzah and `Ali, who both then carried `Ubdaydah bin Harith back to the Muslim camp. `Ubaydah later died from his injuries and he was declared a martyr by the Prophet ﷺ. The Quraysh became nervous and disturbed by seeing their men lose in this way. So, they charged towards the Muslim soldiers angrily, but they were unable to reach the Muslims because they were showered by arrows.

The battle did not last long and the Muslims defeated their enemy. This battle turned out to be deadly for the leaders of the Quraysh because most of them were killed. Abu Jahl and Umayyah bin Khalaf were two of the worst enemies of Islam and they were among those who were killed in the Battle of Badr. At least 70 of the non-believers were killed and another 70 were captured as prisoners.

The Prophet ﷺ allowed the prisoners to buy their freedom by paying a ransom, but those who were the fiercest and harshest enemies of Islam were not allowed to do this; they were put to death instead as a punishment for their crimes. The prisoners who could not pay their ransom were able to buy their freedom by teaching ten Muslim children to read and write.

In this way, the Prophet ﷺ taught his Companions to treat the prisoners of war well. Many of the prisoners who stayed in Madinah became closer to Islam after seeing its beauty because they saw how well they were treated and how the Muslims gave up the best food for them.

The Aftermath of the Battle

Among the prisoners was al-`Abbas, who was also the uncle of Prophet Muhammad ﷺ. Al-`Abbas did not want to fight in the war, but he was forced to do so by the Quraysh. Al-`Abbas was a large man, but he was captured by Abu al-Yasar who was much smaller than him. Prophet Muhammad ﷺ asked Abu al-Yasar how he was able to capture al-`Abbas. "I was able to capture him with the help of a man who I'd never seen before or after," he replied. After Abu al-Yasar described the man's appearance, Prophet Muhammad ﷺ told him that the mystery man was actually an angel.

During the night, while the prisoners were chained up, the Prophet ﷺ could hear the cries of his uncle al-`Abbas. He could not sleep knowing that his uncle was in pain. "O Prophet why are you still awake?" the Companions asked the Prophet ﷺ. "I cannot sleep while I can hear my uncle in pain," the Prophet ﷺ replied. After hearing this, the Companions went to all the prisoners and made sure that none of them was in any difficulty. This was the kind treatment that the Muslims gave to their prisoners.

The next day, the Prophet ﷺ told his uncle al-`Abbas to pay for his freedom and the freedom of his two nephews (Nawfal bin al-Harith and `Aqil bin Abi Talib). `Al-Abbas complained that he did not have any money, but the Prophet ﷺ reminded him of the money that he buried before leaving Makkah and the command that he gave to this wife Umm al-Fadl. He had said to his wife, "If I am killed in this battle, then this money that I have buried is for my children." When al-`Abbas heard this, he said, "By Allah, I know that you are Allah's Messenger, because this is something that nobody except Umm al-Fadl and I knew about."

During the next three days, the Muslims buried the bodies of the Muslims who were martyred in the battle. The bodies of the disbelievers were also gathered, and they were thrown into a large pit. Once all the bodies were buried in the pit, the Prophet ﷺ stood next to it and said, "O people of the pit, have you found what your Lord promised you to be true? For indeed I have found what my Lord has promised to be true." The Companions were amazed at this and asked why the Prophet ﷺ was speaking to the dead. The Prophet ﷺ told them, "You do not hear better than they do, but they cannot reply (to me)." (al-Bukhari)

The Battle of Badr was a great victory for the Muslims, the respect and honour of the Muslims increased greatly, and the reputation of the Quraysh was damaged. The Arabs began to recognise the new founded Muslim state, and saw Madinah as a rising power in Arabia. Before the battle, the enemies of Islam and the hypocrites were certain that the Muslims would be defeated and be destroyed. But this huge victory put awe in their hearts and they realised the strength that was given to the Muslims by Allah.

The Treason of Banu Qaynuqa'

After the Battle of Badr, the Prophet ﷺ returned to Madinah with his Companions. In Madinah, the Prophet ﷺ gathered the Banu Qaynuqa`. The Banu Qaynuqa` were one of the Jewish tribes that had a peace agreement with the Muslims. The Prophet ﷺ said to them, "O Jews, beware of the punishment that came down on the Quraysh. Accept Islam because you know that I am a Prophet sent by Allah, which you have also found written in your holy book."

The Jews of Banu Qaynuqa` responded to the Prophet's invitation to Islam by saying, "O Muhammad, do not be deceived. You fought against people who do not know how to fight, so you were lucky this time. By Allah, if you fight against us, then you will know that we are the ones to fight." The Prophet ﷺ remained silent at their threat. He turned away from them and returned home with his Companions.

The Banu Qaynuqa` were the first Jewish tribe to break the peace agreement with the Muslims. They decided to leave and go to their fortress to teach the Muslims a lesson.

Seven hundred of the Banu Qaynuqa` were in their fortress ready to fight against the Muslims and they hoped that more support would come later from the other Jews. The Prophet ﷺ understood that what they had said earlier was not an empty threat, so he gathered together his Companions and surrounded their fortress with an even greater army. The Banu Qaynuqa ` did not expect that the Muslims could gather such a great force.

Two weeks passed by and no extra support came for the Banu Qaynuqa`. They eventually lost hope and gave themselves up to the Muslims.

The Prophet ﷺ only wanted to stop their threat, so he did not order for any of them to be killed. Instead, he banished them from Madinah. They had to leave immediately and leave all their belongings behind. The Banu Qaynuqa` accepted the option of banishment in exchange for their lives and they moved to north-west Arabia near the borders of Syria.

Lesson 20

Revelation

Wahy is the Arabic word for revelation. A revelation is a direct or indirect message given by Allah to the Prophets. The Prophets passed on Allah's message to their people faithfully and they did not add anything to it or remove anything from it. Allah chooses what He wants to reveal to His Prophets; it could be His commandments, a holy book or a warning to a people of a punishment that was coming.

Not all human beings can receive Allah's revelation. Only the Prophets can receive it because they are chosen by Allah. It is only through them that we receive Allah's commands and message. There are different ways in which Allah speaks to His Prophets, and they are all different forms of revelation.

They are:

1. INSPIRATION

This is a direct message Allah places in the heart of the Prophets. Sometimes this can come in the form of a true dream.

2. ALLAH'S SPEECH FROM BEHIND A VEIL

The Prophets hear Allah, but they do not see Him. However, they understand whatever Allah says to them.

3. RECEIVING ALLAH'S MESSAGE THROUGH AN ANGEL

This is an indirect form of revelation. Allah sends His message to the Prophets and Messengers through the means of an angel, such as Angel Jibra'il.

The Past Revelations

Allah revealed Holy Books and Scrolls to the Messengers before Prophet Muhammad ﷺ, and it is obligatory for us to believe in all of them. These Holy Books and Scrolls contained Allah's speech which He revealed to the Messengers. Sometimes they came down in a book form or they were passed on by an angel. Belief in the Holy Books and Scrolls that came before Islam is an important part of our religion; we cannot be Muslims without it.

The following books and scrolls were revealed to the past Prophets:

1. AT-TAWRAH (THE TORAH)

This book was revealed to Prophet Musa عليه السلام. The Tawrah was a book of laws. Prophet

Musa ﷺ and the Prophets after him used the laws revealed in the Tawrah to judge the people of Bani Isra'il.

2. AL-INJIL (THE GOSPEL)

This book was revealed to Prophet `Isa ﷺ. The Injil contained laws supporting the laws that were written in the Tawrah before it. However, it also brought some new laws for the people of Bani Isra'il and cancelled some old ones from the Tawrah.

3. AZ-ZABUR (THE PSALMS)

This was a book Allah revealed to Prophet Dawud ﷺ. The Zabur was not a book of law. It was a book of hymns, prayers and glorifications, which Allah taught Prophet Dawud ﷺ. Allah did not reveal any rules in this book.

4. The Scrolls of Prophet Ibrahim عليه السلام and Prophet Musa عليه السلام.

We must believe in the above books and scrolls because they were revealed by Allah. They all contained Allah's words. The message of all the holy Books and Scrolls was one: to worship Allah and not to associate any partners with Him. They were only different in some of the laws given by Allah.

Unfortunately, none of the previous revelations are with us today in their original form. Some of them were written down but then became lost and others were changed by their people.

The Final Revelation: The Qur'an

Allah revealed the Qur'an to Prophet Muhammad ﷺ, His last and final Prophet and Messenger. It is a book of law and guidance and it confirms the original message of all the past books and revelations.

The Qur'an is the final source of guidance for people. The past books were only for one community and not for everybody, but the Qur'an is for everyone, human beings and the Jinn alike. Due to its greatness and perfection, it is Allah's final revelation and there will be no revelation after it. The door of revelation closed with the passing of Prophet Muhammad ﷺ, and this door will never be opened again. No person can claim that they are a Prophet or that they have received a revelation after Prophet Muhammad ﷺ.

As the Qur'an is the last and final revelation, Allah promised to protect it from any change. The Qur'an today is the same as it was at the time of revelation and no change has been made to it. For this reason, we are only allowed to worship Allah through the Qur'an and not through the earlier books, because all the earlier holy books have been replaced by the Qur'an.

The Greatest Miracle

The Qur'an is not only the speech of Allah; it is also the greatest miracle of Prophet Muhammad ﷺ, which came as a challenge to all humanity. During the 7th century, the Arabs had become very good at speaking the Arabic

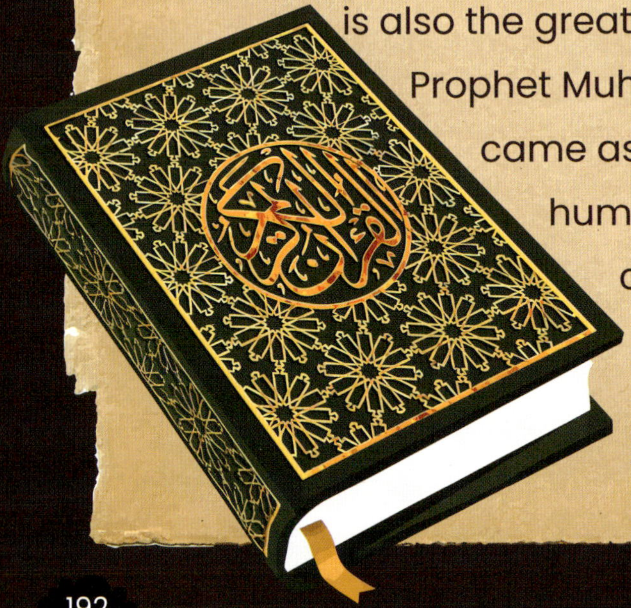

language. This time in Arab history produced some of the best poets. The Qur'an came in this time when the Arabic language was at its highest.

The Qur'an challenged the disbelieving Arabs. If they believed that the Qur'an is not Allah's revelation to Prophet Muhammad ﷺ, then they should produce a Qur'an like it. But the disbelieving Arabs could not do it. So, Allah made the challenge easier and told them to produce ten chapters like the Qur'an, but again they could not do it. So, Allah made the challenge easier still, and asked them to produce one chapter like the Qur'an, but again the disbelieving Arabs were unable to produce even one chapter, the shortest of which is three verses!

There were many great poets among the Arabs, but they were unable to write anything that was equal to the Qur'an's beautiful Arabic.

Instead of accepting this challenge, they started to harm the Muslims. They drove the Muslims out of their homes and forced them to emigrate to Madinah. They even spent a lot of their money just to fight wars against the Muslims, and some of them even lost their lives and sons in these battles.

If they wanted to stop Islam, all they had to do was respond to the challenge. They did not have to go through all this difficulty and choose the hard way when a simple and straight-forward option was available to them. But they knew that they could not respond to the challenge, because the Qur'an was not written by any human being; it was the revelation of Allah. More than 1400 years have passed and yet no one has been able to meet this challenge, and no one ever will.

Lesson 21

The Friday Prayer

Different religions have their own holy days. In Judaism, Saturday is the holy day and it is known as the 'Sabbath'. In Christianity, Sunday is the holy day as it is the day of rest; Christians attend the church on this day. For Muslims, the holy day is Friday (Jumu`ah) and it is the best day of the week. This is the day when Prophet Adam عليه السلام was created and it will be the day when the Day of Judgement will take place (Muslim).

Prophet Muhammad ﷺ taught us to perform the following actions on a Friday:

- We should have a bath, put on perfume and wear our best clothes.
- We should recite salutations on the Prophet ﷺ (Salat `ala an-Nabi ﷺ).

- We should recite Surat al-Kahf.
- We make du`a to Allah because there is an hour on this day when the du`a is accepted.
- We should go to the mosque to perform the Friday prayer (Salat al-Jumu`ah) in congregation and listen to the Imam's sermon (khutbah).

The Friday prayer (Salat al-Jumu`ah) is two units of prayer. It is performed at the time of the Zuhr prayer. Instead of the four units of the fard prayer, we replace it with the two khutbahs (sermons) of the Imam and the two units of the Friday prayer. The four fard of the Zuhr prayer in turn becomes a Sunnah Mu`akkadah prayer, which is emphasised and important to offer. If someone misses the Friday prayer (Salat al-Jumu`ah), they should offer the Zuhr prayer in its place.

The table on the following page shows us the units of the Friday prayer.

Sunnah	Fard	Sunnah	Sunnah	Nafl
4	2	4	2	2

We should try our best to get to the mosque as early as possible. The earlier we get there, the more reward we get. We should try to fill the front rows nearest to the Imam first and fill in the gaps in the rows in front of us.

The following is a step-by-step guide of what takes place during the Friday prayer (Salat al-Jumu`ah).

Step-by-Step Guide

1. The Muezzin makes the first Adhan. This Adhan is to tell everyone to stop what they are doing and to come to the mosque to perform the Friday prayer (Salat al-Jumu`ah),

2. We perform the four units of the Sunnah Mu`akkadah prayer and then we wait quietly for the Imam to deliver the sermon (khutbah). In some mosques, the Imam (or a speaker) may give a talk while everyone is waiting.

3. When the Imam is ready to deliver the sermon (khutbah), he will go up the pulpit (minbar) and sit there facing the congregation (jama`ah). When the Imam sits on the pulpit (minbar), we should complete any prayer that we need to perform and be prepared to listen to the Imam's sermon (khutbah)

4. The second Adhan is recited.

5. The Imam will stand up and deliver the first sermon (khutbah). During the sermon (khutbah), we must not talk or get distracted. We are not

allowed to say Salam to anyone or even tell someone off for talking.

6. The Imam will sit down. This is a time to make a supplication (du`a) to Allah quietly. It is a time when Allah accepts the supplications.

7. The Imam will then deliver the second sermon (khutbah). At the end of this sermon, the Imam will recite some supplications and we should say 'Ameen' to them quietly.

8. After the sermons are finished, the iqamah will be recited, and the Imam will lead the two unit

prayer for the Friday Prayer (Salat al-Jumu`ah) in congregation.

9. After the Friday prayer we perform the rest of the units of the Friday prayer on our own. They are the following prayers in this order: the four unit Sunnah Mu`akkadah prayer, the two unit Sunnah Mu`akkadah prayer and the two unit Nafl prayer

This completes the Friday prayer
(Salat al-Jumu`ah).

After the prayer, we should meet our brothers and sisters in our community. This is a time to talk to other Muslims. Friday is a day when we should send salutations on Prophet Muhammad ﷺ (Salat `ala an-Nabi ﷺ). In some mosques, this is recited together in a beautiful tune after the Friday prayer.

Lesson 22

Life After Death

When the time of death comes, the Angel of Death, Izra'il, will come to take our soul. Death is not the end, but it is the beginning of a new life in the Barzakh (the Interspace). The Barzakh is a realm which is between this life and the next. It is a place where the soul will remain until the Day of Judgement. In the Barzakh, the soul will either receive reward or punishment depending on the deeds it performed in this worldly life.

Let us read about the journey of the soul at the time of death.

The Good Soul

When a good person is on the deathbed, the angels of mercy descend from the heavens and they surround that person as he is dying. These angels will have beautiful and radiant faces that shine bright like the sun. They will fill the horizon as far as the eye can see and they will bring with them a cloth from Paradise and some perfume. Then the Angel of Death will come until he sits beside the dying person's head. He will say, "O pure soul! Come out to the forgiveness and pleasure of Allah."

Hearing this, the soul will rise from the body with ease like the way a drop of water flows from the mouth of a bottle. As the soul leaves the body, the Angel of Death will take it quickly, and the other angels will take it from him quickly before the blink of an eye. They then wrap the soul in the Heavenly cloth mixed in with the perfume, and when the soul is taken out of the cloth, a fragrance comes from it like the sweetest smelling perfume found on the face of the earth.

The angels then take the soul and ascend with it to the Heavens. Every time they pass a gathering of angels, they ask, "Who is this good soul?' The angels reply, "It is so-and-so, the son of so-and-so." They will mention the best names he was addressed with in the world. When they cross this earthly realm, they will ask for the gates of the heavens to be opened for the good soul and the gates will be opened for it.

The angels will keep on ascending through the heavens with the good soul until they reach the seventh heaven. Then the good soul will be brought to the presence of its Lord. Allah will say, "Register the book of My slave in `Illiyin (a station of Paradise) and return him to the earth. For I created him from it and to it I shall make him return. And I will make him come from it another time."

The good soul will then be brought back to the earth to its body. When it returns, it sees the washing of its body, its shrouding and the funeral procession, and it says, "Take me forward! Take me forward!"

When the body has been placed in the grave, the two angels Munkar and Nakir come into the grave and sit beside it. They ask, "Who is your Lord?" The good soul will reply, "My Lord is Allah." They will then ask, "What is your religion?" The good soul will reply, "My religion is Islam." Then they will ask,

"Who is this man who was raised among you?" The good soul will reply, "He is Muhammad, the Messenger of Allah." Then they will ask, "How did you come to know about this?" And the good soul will reply, "I read the Book of Allah and I believed in it."

Then a voice from the Heavens will declare, "My servant has spoken the truth. So, spread out a carpet from Paradise and clothe him in heavenly garments. And open for him a door to Heaven." Then his or her grave is made bigger to as far as the eye can see.

A man with beautiful garments and a fragrant scent comes to him and says, "Celebrate in what delights you for this is the day which you were promised." The deceased person asks, "Who are you? Yours is a face which brings good." He replies, "I am your good deeds." Then he will say, "O My Lord, let the Hour come soon so that I may join my family!"

The Bad Soul

When a bad person is on the deathbed, the angels from the Hellfire come and surround the person as he is dying. These angels will have dark and gloomy faces and they will fill the horizon as far as the eye can see. They will bring with them a rough hair-cloth. Then the Angel of Death will come until he sits beside the dying person's head. He will say, "O foul soul! Come out to the wrath and anger of Allah."

Hearing this, the soul will scatter within the body, but it will be dragged out like a spike is pulled out of wet wool. As the soul is ripped out of the body, the Angel of Death will take it quickly, and the other angels will take it from him quickly before the blink of an eye. They then wrap the soul in the rough hair-cloth and a disgusting smell comes out of it like the worse stench of a corpse on the face of the earth.

The angels then take the soul and ascend with it to the Heavens. Every time they pass a gathering of angels, they ask, "Who is this foul soul?" The angels will reply, "It is so-and-so, the son of so-and-so." They will mention the ugliest names he was addressed with in the world. When they cross this earthly realm, they will ask for the gates of the heavens to be opened for the bad soul, but the gates will not be opened.

Allah will say, "Register the book of My slave in Sijjin (Hell) in the lowest earth." Then the bad soul will be thrown out. It will fall through the heavens until it reaches its body on Earth. When it returns, it sees the washing of its body, its shrouding and the funeral procession, and it will say, "Where are you taking me?"

When the body has been placed in the grave, the two angels Munkar and Nakir come into the grave, sit beside the deceased and ask, "Who is your Lord?"

The bad soul will reply, "Alas, alas, I do not know." They will then ask, "What is your religion?" He will say, "Alas, alas, I do not know." Then they will ask, "Who is this man who was raised among you?" And he will reply, "Alas, alas, I do not know."

Then a voice from the Heavens will declare, "He has lied. So, spread out a carpet from the Hellfire and open for him one of its doors." They will open a door for him and he will feel its blast. His grave will be narrowed so much that his ribs will be pressed together.

An ugly man with the most hideous face and the most horrible stench will come to him and he will say, "Suffer because of what has brought you disgrace for this is the day which you were promised." The deceased person will ask, "Who are you? Yours is a face which brings evil." He replies, "I am your bad deeds." Then he will say, "O My Lord, let the Hour not come!"

Lesson 23

The Eid Prayers

There are other congregational prayers which are necessary (Wajib) for Muslims to perform. These include the two Eid prayers (Salat al-`Id). The Eid prayers are annual prayers because they both come once a year. Eid al-Fitr takes place on the first day of Shawwal, after completing a month of fasting in Ramadan. Eid al-Adha takes place on the 10th of Dhu al-Hijjah, when the Pilgrims make a sacrifice and remove their Ihram.

On the two days of Eid, we perform a two unit Eid prayer (Salat al-`Id) followed by listening to two sermons (khutbah) delivered by the Imam. The Eid prayer (Salat al-`Id) is performed after sunrise in the morning.

On the day of Eid, it is Sunnah for us to do the following actions:

- Have a bath and brush one's teeth.
- Put on perfume.
- Wear one's best clothes (even if they are not new).
- On Eid al-Fitr, eat something sweet before leaving to offer the prayer. (It is recommended to eat an odd number of dates.)
- On Eid al-Adha, do not eat anything until you have returned from the prayer.

- Recite the following takbir on the way to the prayer:

Allaahu Akbar Allaahu Akbar. Laa ilaaha illallaahu wallaahu akbar. Allaahu akbar wa lillaahil hamd.

اَللّٰهُ أَكْبَرُ اَللّٰهُ أَكْبَرُ. لَا إِلٰهَ إِلَّا اللّٰهُ وَاللّٰهُ أَكْبَرُ.
اَللّٰهُ أَكْبَرُ وَلِلّٰهِ الْحَمْدُ

Allah is the greatest; Allah is the greatest. There is no god but Allah. Allah is the greatest; Allah is the greatest; and all praise belongs to Allah.

This takbir should be recited quietly on Eid al-Fitr and loudly on Eid al-Adha.

- Walk to the Eid prayer. We should use one route to go to the prayer and a different route on the way back. This was the practice of Prophet Muhammad ﷺ.

The two units of the Eid prayer (Salat al-`Id) is a Wajib prayer which has six extra takbirs. We raise our hands in each of the takbirs, but we do not fold our arms in between them. There is no Adhan or Iqamah for this prayer.

The way to perform the Eid prayer (Salat al-`Id) is mentioned below.

How to Offer the Eid Prayer (Salat al-`Id)

1. Begin by facing the Qiblah and perform the intention to perform the two units of Salat al-`Id behind the Imam, with six extra Takbirs.

2. Perform the Takbir at-Tahrimah.

3. Perform the Qiyam (the Standing Position) and fold the arms

placing the right hand over the left.

4. First recite the Thana' (Praise of Allah).

5. Then perform three extra Takbirs (saying 'Allaahu Akbar') by raising the hand each time. Do not fold the arms during the Takbir; keep your arms relaxed as in the Qawmah (the Short Standing Position).

6. After performing the additional Takbirs, fold your arms again. The Imam will recite the Ta`awwudh (Seeking Refuge in Allah) and then the Tasmiyah (In the Name of Allah) silently.

7. Then listen to the Imam recite Surat al-Fatihah followed by a Surah.

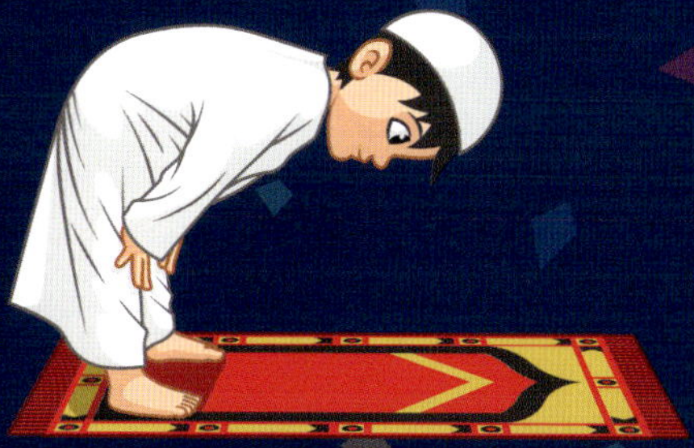

8. Perform the Ruku' (the Bowing Position).

9. Perform the Qawmah (the Short Standing Position).

10. Perform the Sajdah (the First Prostration Position).

11. Perform the Jalsah (the Short Sitting Position).

12. Perform the Sajdah (the Second Prostration Position).

13. Then return to the second unit by performing the Qiyam (the Standing Position). Listen to the Imam recite Surat al-Fatihah followed by a Surah.

14. Perform three more extra Takbirs (saying 'Allaahu Akbar') by raising the hand each time. Do not fold the arms in between; keep them relaxed.

15. After the third extra Takbir, keeping the hands placed on each side, go straight into the Ruku' (the Bowing Position) after the Imam.

16. Perform the Qawmah (the Short Standing Position).

17. Perform the Sajdah (the First Prostration Position).

18. Perform the Jalsah (the Short Sitting Position).

19. Perform the Sajdah (the Second Prostration Position).

20. Perform the Qa'dah (the Sitting Position). Recite the Tashahhud (the Bearing Testimony). Then recite the Salat Ibrahimiyya (Abrahamic Salutation) followed by a Du`a.

21. Then end the prayer by performing the Salam (The Ending Position).

22. Stay sitting down after the prayer. The Imam will get up and sit on the pulpit (minbar). He will deliver the first sermon (khutbah). We should listen to this quietly and not make any noise or talk.

23. The Imam will sit down, and he will get up again to recite the second sermon (khutbah). We should listen to this quietly. At the end of the sermon, the Imam will make a supplication (du`a) to Allah, and we should say 'Ameen' quietly to the supplication.

This completes the Eid prayer (Salat al-`Id).

After the prayer, we should meet our fellow brothers and sisters in Islam. We should shake the hands of our brother/sister and greet them saying

Eid Mubarak (Blessed Eid!) or Eid Sa`id (Happy Eid!). This is a time to spend with family and friends; we should not be busy in performing extra Nafl prayers before or after the Eid prayers because we should be spending time with our community and family on the day of Eid.

Friday is also an Eid for the Muslims (Ibn Majah), but unlike the two days of Eid, it is a weekly Eid and not an annual one.

Lesson 24

Sirah: The Battle of Uhud

As soon as Abu Sufyan returned home safely with his trade caravan, the Quraysh met together to plan their revenge against the Muslims. They agreed to use the wealth from the caravan for this purpose. Jubayr bin Mut`am had an Abyssinian slave called Wahshi, who was an expert in throwing the spear. He promised Wahshi that he would set him free if he killed Hamzah, the Prophet's uncle. Jubayr wanted revenge because Hamzah killed his father in the battle of Badr. Abu Sufyan's wife Hind also promised to give him her jewellery because she wanted revenge for the death of her father `Utbah, uncle Shaybah and her brother Walid.

When news reached Madinah that the Quraysh were planning another attack, the Prophet ﷺ

gathered the Muslims together to have a meeting about the approaching battle. The Prophet's opinion was that they should remain in Madinah and fight the Quraysh from within the city. `Abd Allah bin Ubayy, who was one of the hypocrites (someone who says they are a Muslim, but they are not in reality), also had this opinion, but the Muslims wanted to go out and meet the enemies head on. The Prophet ﷺ saw the enthusiasm of his Companions and so he agreed to going out of Madinah to fight.

The Prophet ﷺ put on his armour and helmet and got his sword ready. When the Companions saw the Prophet ﷺ getting ready for war, they felt sorry that they made the Prophet ﷺ follow their suggestion of leaving Madinah. They said that they would remain in Madinah and fight the Quraysh from within the city. But the Prophet ﷺ was not

upset by this. He said, "It is not suitable for a Prophet to put on his armour for war and then take it off until Allah has judged between him and his enemies."
So, the Muslims left Madinah with an army of one thousand soldiers and camped at the foot of Mount Uhud, which was north of Madinah.

The Hypocrites Betrayal

On their way to Uhud, the hypocrite `Abd Allah bin Ubayy decided to turn back and return to Madinah with 300 of his soldiers, who like him were also hypocrites. He complained that the Prophet ﷺ did not listen to him about fighting from within Madinah, and so he felt that he had no reason to leave Madinah and help in the battle. This move from `Abd Allah bin Ubayy was a great act of betrayal and disloyalty. One of the Companions followed him and called out to him, telling him not to abandon the Prophet ﷺ at a time when he was facing his enemies. But the leader of the hypocrites, Ibn Ubayy, ignored him and kept on walking back towards Madinah.

After losing 300 soldiers, the 1000 strong Muslim army was now reduced to 700. The Muslims were concerned and asked the Prophet ﷺ to call the Jewish tribes of Madinah to come out and defend their city. But the Prophet ﷺ reassured his Companions that there was no need to worry and that there was no need to ask for help.

However, a Jewish rabbi called Mukhayriq came out to fight. He reminded the Jewish tribes to follow the peace agreement with the Muslims and to protect Madinah from its enemies, but they ignored him. Mukhayriq was martyred in this battle, and the Prophet ﷺ declared that he was the best of the Jews.

The Two Armies Meet

When the Muslims reached Mount Uhud, the Prophet ﷺ placed fifty archers on a hill near the Muslim army. He chose `Abd Allah bin Jubayr to supervise the fifty archers and commanded them to attack any horsemen that tried to attack the Muslims from behind. He gave them strict orders to not move from their place, whether they were winning or losing. Their job was to remain on this hill until they received further orders.

The Quraysh had arrived with an army of 3000 men with an extra 200 horsemen. Their army was much bigger than the Muslim army which numbered only 700. This time the Quraysh also brought their women with them, among them was the wife of Abu Sufyan, Hind bint `Utbah, who had promised to take revenge for her family that was killed at Badr. She recited verses of poetry and the other women beat drums to encourage the men to fight.

The Fighting Begins

When the battle started, the Muslims fought in neat rows whereas the non-believers came charging like an angry crowd. The horsemen remained behind on both sides. On the left side, near the small hill where the Muslim archers were, Khalid bin Walid tried to lead his soldiers to attack the Muslims from behind, but he was stopped with a shower of arrows from the archers.

The battle continued and many important members of the Quraysh such as Talhah from the Banu `Abd al-Dar tribe were killed. Talhah was the person who carried the flag of the Quraysh. His two brothers and four sons were also killed on this day, as each of them took the flag of the Quraysh after another got killed.

However, this day was also deadly for the Muslims, as Wahshi made his way from the edge of the battlefield to find Hamzah. He watched and waited for the moment that would win him his freedom.

When he was close enough, he threw his spear and hit Hamzah below the armpit and into his belly. He had killed Hamzah, the Prophet's uncle. Wahshi then left the battlefield and waited for the fight to be over.

Even with the loss of Hamzah, the Muslims continued to fight bravely and broke the positions of their enemies until they could see the camps of the Quraysh on the other side. The Quraysh were now weakened, and the enemy soldiers started to run away from the battlefield. It looked like victory was certain for the Muslims. Many Muslims started to go to the enemy camps to get hold of the gains of war.

The Battle Swings in the Quraysh's Favour

The fifty archers that were commanded to stay in their place began coming down from the hill because they thought that the battle was over. `Abd Allah bin Jubayr called out to them telling them to not leave their positions, but they did not pay any attention to him. Only ten archers remained on the hill.

When this happened, Khalid bin Walid saw his chance and he led his soldiers from behind the hill and attacked the Muslim army from behind. The Muslims were now stuck in the middle with the enemy on both sides.

The enemy soldiers who had left the battlefield, now returned and started fighting with determination because they saw that the archers abandoned their position, and now the Muslims were not organised anymore and were being forced to find shelter.

The Muslim soldiers were being cut down one by one by the enemy horsemen. The enemy was now close enough to attack the Prophet ﷺ. The ten archers who remained on the hill were all martyred, and the Muslim army began to feel weaker against the larger and stronger enemy.

The Muslims were forced to climb up Mount Uhud, using it to shield their backs. A sharp stone was thrown in the Prophet's direction, and it hit the Prophet's blessed lips. Blood was pouring out and it covered the Prophet's blessed face. The injury was so severe that it broke one of the Prophet's tooth. The Prophet ﷺ reassured his Companions that he was alright, and they continued fighting.

There was a dangerous point in the battle as the enemy soldiers reached close to the Prophet ﷺ and only a small group of Companions were surrounding him to fight them off. Many Companions gave their lives on this day or were seriously injured during the fighting. They fought till the end to keep the Prophet ﷺ safe from the enemies.

The Quraysh Target the Prophet ﷺ

A female Companion called Nusaybah bint Ka`b was one of the Companions who fought bravely to protect the Prophet ﷺ. She was one of the two women from Madinah who pledged her allegiance at the Second Pledge of al-`Aqabah. During the battle, when the Muslims were being attacked from all directions, she picked up a sword and arrows and fought the enemies. She fired arrows at the enemy and killed many of them. Remembering her bravery, the Prophet ﷺ said, "Wherever I turned on the Day of Uhud, I saw her fighting for me."

The Companions fought bravely on this day but even then, one of the horsemen from the Quraysh was able to get close to the Prophet ﷺ. He came charging at the Prophet ﷺ with his sword. As he got close to the Prophet ﷺ, the horseman brought down his sword with full force towards the Prophet's helmet, but it was moved away by a Companion who used his hand as a shield. The sword narrowly missed the Prophet's helmet. It grazed the side of the helmet and struck the Prophet's shoulder, which was protected by his armour.

This blow from the enemy soldier was severe, and for a moment the Prophet ﷺ fell to the ground. Seeing this, the horseman quickly rode back and shouted at the top of his voice that the Prophet ﷺ had been killed! This news brought great sadness to the Muslims. The Quraysh thought that they had completed their task and had taken their revenge for those who were killed at the battle of Badr, and so they relaxed their effort and started backing away.

Some of the Muslims who believed that the Prophet ﷺ had been killed, did not want to live without him, so they kept on fighting until they were martyred. There was a lot of sadness within the Muslim army and the archers who left their position on the hill were extremely upset by this news.

However the Prophet ﷺ regained his strength and got up. When the Muslims saw that the Prophet ﷺ was alive, they were greatly relieved. They went into a small opening in Mount Uhud and remained there.

After Uhud

The battle had come to an end, and the Quraysh felt happy and triumphant. Abu Sufyan came over to the Muslims and spoke about his happiness that they had taken revenge for the battle of Badr. He said, "War goes by turns, and this day for a day. Exalted be Hubal, may his religion prevail." The Prophet ﷺ commanded `Umar bin al-Khattab to reply to him and say, "Allah is the Highest and Supreme. We are not equal. Our martyrs are in Paradise and yours are in the Hellfire." Abu Sufyan then asked `Umar if the news of the Prophet's killing was true. `Umar replied that it was not. Hearing this, Abu Sufyan turned away and returned to his camp.

While the Quraysh were gathering their dead bodies, Hind bint `Utbah asked Wahshi to show her where the dead body of Hamzah was. She asked for Hamzah's liver to be cut out of his body and she took a bite out of it and swallowed it. The other women of the Quraysh started cutting off the nose and ears of the Muslim soldiers and made necklaces from them to keep as a trophies of their victory.

After the Quraysh left the battlefield, the Prophet ﷺ and his Companions spent the next three days burying the martyrs. They were very saddened to see the bodies of their brothers damaged by the non-believers.

They buried the Companions and performed the funeral prayers for them. It was a day of sadness as many Muslims had been killed on this day. When they returned to Madinah, many families were mourning their lost ones. Even though it was an extremely sad day for the Muslims, they all thanked Allah and praised him for everything, especially for keeping His beloved Prophet Muhammad ﷺ alive and safe.

Lesson 25

The Day of Judgement

Allah created us for a reason. He has put us in this world because this life is a test. Compared to the next life, which will be everlasting, this life is very short, and it is only one stop in our long journey to our final home (Paradise or Hell). All the choices that we make in this life will have consequences in the next. So, we must be very careful with the choices that we make because we will be asked about them.

Like everything in this universe, one day this world will come to an end. There will be a last day when the world will be destroyed. This last day is called the 'Day of Judgement'. Only Allah knows when the Day of Judgement will take place. However, it is our duty as Muslims to prepare for this day, because it will be the day when we meet Allah.

On the Day of Judgement, Allah will create the earth again and He will bring us back to life. We will then be brought before Allah to answer for our choices, because Allah sees everything that we do and hears everything that we say. This will be the day when Allah will judge our actions, tell us what we did in the world and decide whether we have been good in this life.

Allah will not let our actions go to waste. Every good deed that we do will be rewarded by Him and every bad deed that we do will be punished, unless He forgives us for it. When people do evil in this world and harm other people, but they are not punished in this life, then on the Day of Judgement they will be answerable to Allah and they will be punished. If we do not try to do the right things in this life, then on the Last Day Allah will question us about it.

The following are the great events that will take place on the Day of Judgement.

The Blowing of the Trumpet

Allah created the Trumpet and He has commanded Angel Israfil to blow it at the fixed time. Ever since Angel Israfil was given this duty, he does nothing but keep the trumpet to his lips and wait for the order to blow. He does not even blink in case the order to blow the trumpet is given to him and he misses it. On Allah's command, Angel Israfil will blow the Trumpet and the Day of Judgement will take place. It will come as a surprise to the people of the future, when it will take place, because it will happen suddenly.

The Resurrection

Angel Israfil will blow the Trumpet twice. The first blow will destroy everything, and all the living creatures on the earth will die. After the first blow, Allah will create everything again at the appointed time. Allah will then command Angel Israfil to blow the Trumpet for a second time, and this will bring all the dead back to life.

Allah will recreate everyone's body perfectly as it was during their life and then He will place the soul back into the new body. This coming to life after dying is called the resurrection. When everyone is alive again, they will be brought to the mahshar (the gathering place), where everyone will be questioned for their deeds in their life in this world.

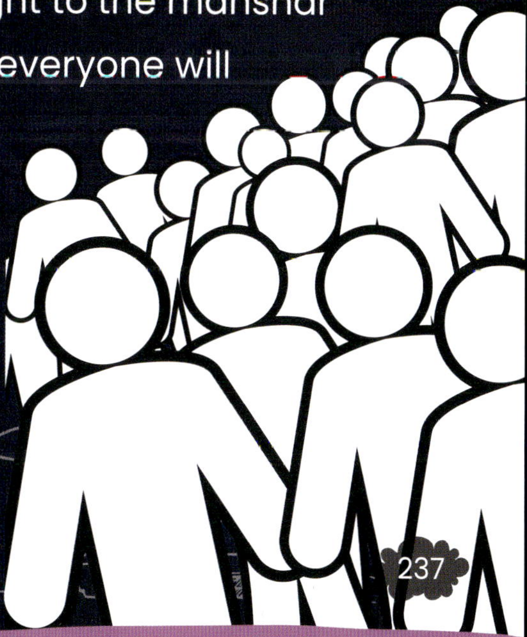

The Gathering Place (Mahshar)

After the resurrection, everyone will be brought to the gathering place (mahshar). At this gathering place, all human beings, from the first to the last, will be made to stand before Allah. The sun will be very close to the heads of the people. Anyone who is not under the shade of Allah's `Arsh (Throne) will be sweating very much, so much that some people will be drowning in their own sweat, and others will have sweat reaching up to their ankles or shoulders.

At the gathering place, Allah will tell everyone the truth about the things they did not agree on. On this day, good will be distiguished from evil. The Prophets and their followers will be proven right. It will be on this day that everyone will know the reality of the events that took place on the earth, and the truth, even if it was hidden from everyone, will come out in the open.

The Weighing of the Deeds

On the Day of Judgment, everyone's deeds will be weighed to see whose good deeds outweighed their bad deeds. Those whose scales will weigh heavy due to the good deeds will be successful on that day. And those whose scales will be light due to the little weight of goods deeds will be unsuccessful.

After the weighing of the deeds, everyone will then be given their book of deeds. These books contain a record of everyone's actions. The righteous people will get their book of deeds in their right hand, but the evildoers will receive their book in the left. The good people will want everyone to read their book, but the wicked people will try to hide their book and will not want others to look at it.

Crossing the Bridge (Sirat)

After this, the believers will be made to cross the bridge over Hell; the bridge is called the 'Sirat'. No one knows the reality of the Sirat, but it is reported to be thinner than a hair, sharper than a sword and surrounded by pitch-black darkness. The more good deeds a person has, the easier it will be for them to cross it. Some of the believers will cross the Sirat as quickly as the wink of an eye, some others as quick as lightning, a strong wind or a fast horse. The more good deeds a person does in this life the easier it will be to cross the Sirat, and the less good deeds a person does the harder it will become.

Some believers will not make it across the Sirat and they will fall into the Hellfire. They will then remain inside the Hellfire until the Prophet ﷺ comes to help them. The Prophet ﷺ will pray to Allah and intercede for them to be saved from the Hellfire.

The Journey's End

Those believers who will cross the Sirat safely to the other side will be saved from the Hellfire and they will then make their way to Paradise. All the difficulties and hardships of the Day of Judgement will be behind them. The Prophet ﷺ will meet the Muslims at the Fountain of al-Kawthar, which will be a great gift from Allah. Whoever drinks from this fountain will never feel thirsty again.

The Prophet ﷺ will then lead his Ummah to Paradise and he will knock on its door. The doors of Paradise will be opened for him and then his Ummah will enter it. Once they enter its gates, they will never experience any hardship or worry ever again. In fact, they will forget all the problems they had ever experienced in their earthly life. They will be young and beautiful, and their faces will be glowing like the bright moon.

In Paradise, the Muslims will see Allah for the first time. This will be the happiest moment for the believers and it will be the ending of our long and difficult journey. Everything a believer does in this life is for this one moment. Allah did not create us to be lost in the pleasures and delights of this life or the next, but He created us to be with Him, to love Him and to enjoy His nearness forever.

May Allah bless us with this meeting – the moment when we see Him for the first time. Amin!

Lesson 26

Halal and Haram (Part One)

One of the meanings of Islam is '**submission (to God)**'. This means that we follow everything that Allah (God) has told us to do and we do not disobey Him.

Allah (God) has given us laws to follow so that we may live morally (by doing the right thing). When we submit to God we follow these laws. Allah is the All-Knowing and the Most-Wise, He knows what is best for us. He knows what the best rules and guidelines are for us to follow. If we want to live a virtuous (good) life, we must obey these laws because they are there to help us. By following them, our life will be full of goodness and blessings.

Allah has set limits for us which we cannot go past. As long as we stay within these limits, we are following the rules of Allah. Everything that falls within the limits is known as '**halal**' (**lawful**). If something is lawful, it means that we are allowed to do it. Whatever is outside of the boundaries is known as '**haram**' (**unlawful**), and when something is unlawful it means that we are not allowed to do it.

The best way to follow the rules of Allah is to follow the **Sunnah of the Prophet** ﷺ. The Sunnah is the practice of Prophet Muhammad ﷺ. It is how he lived his life. The Prophet ﷺ showed us how to follow the rules of Allah. Through his Sunnah he explained the Qur'an. His life is a practical example of the Qur'an. Through the Sunnah, we understand the Qur'an better and we learn the true way to follow Allah's rules in our life.

The Mother of the Believers `A'isha said that the behaviour of the Prophet ﷺ was the Qur'an (Ahmad). Everything the Prophet ﷺ said or did was his Sunnah. We must follow the Sunnah of the Prophet ﷺ in our life because his Sunnah is what brings us closer to Allah. The Prophet ﷺ is Allah's favourite and beloved servant; if we want to be close to Allah, then we must walk in his footsteps and follow his example.

Allah put His rules in the Qur'an and the Sunnah of Prophet Muhammad ﷺ. If we follow the Qur'an and Sunnah, it means we are following Allah's rules. Every part of our life is included in Allah's rules, from the food that we eat, the things that we wear and the things that we do in our everyday life.

There are many more things that are halal (lawful) than those that are haram (unlawful). By learning what is haram (unlawful) first, we can easily work out what is halal (lawful). The haram (unlawful) things are the limits that Allah has placed for us and we should not go near these limits.

Personal Dealings

Allah has set limits in the way that we treat one another. We are not allowed to bring harm to ourselves or our body. We cannot hurt others and cause them to be in pain or to worry. We cannot harm anyone. Doing these things is unlawful (haram) and we must stay away from them. If someone does any of these things, they have taken part in a major sin, and they must ask Allah for forgiveness.

Some examples of Allah's limits and the major sins are the following:

1. Killing/Committing Murder
2. Disrespecting Parents
3. Using Black-Magic
4. Gambling
5. Stealing
6. Hitting or treating someone bad
7. Taking wealth from orphans
8. Breaking promises

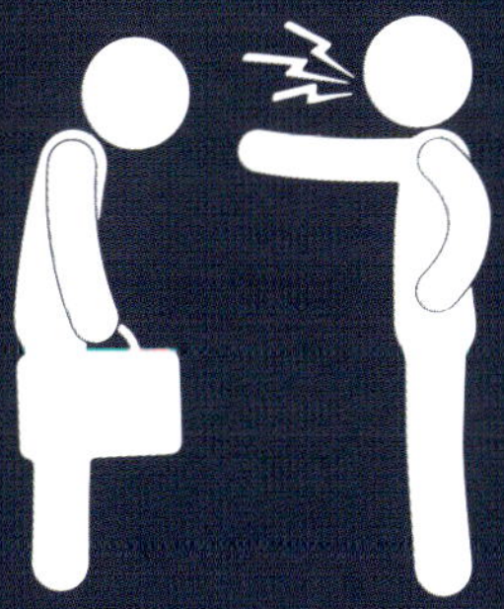

9. Treating animals badly

The limits of Allah are not just about our outward actions that we do, they also include our inward actions like the way that we think. Our thinking must also be within the limits of Allah. Thinking that you are better than others and looking down at other people is a major sin.

Speech

From all of creation Allah has given humans the ability to speak. Having speech is a great blessing as well as a great responsibility. Allah will question us on the Day of Judgement about the things that we said, and also the things that we did in this life.

If we control our tongue and use it only for saying good things, we will be successful in this life and the next. But if we use our tongue to say bad things about other people and to hurt their feelings, then we will be held responsible for it. On the Day of

Insulting Others
Gossiping
Lying
Cursing
Slander
Backbiting

Judgement, Allah will give our good deeds to the person that we hurt and if we have no good deeds to give, then their bad deeds will be given to us.

Some of the limits of the tongue and the major sins are:

The limits of the tongue are not just to do with the things that we say. It also includes the things that we write on the internet or through text messaging. We have to be just as careful with our social media accounts as we are with our tongues when we speak. The things that we write to our friends and family, and others, through our computers and mobile phones, should be good and pleasing to Allah.

Clothing

We wear clothes to cover our body and to beautify ourselves. Allah has given us limits about the way that we dress. Some of the limits which we have to keep in mind are the following:

1. The clothes we wear should cover the body properly. Boys must cover everything between the belly button and the knees. Girls must cover all parts of the body except for the face, hands and feet.

2. The clothing we wear must not be too tight or revealing. It needs to be loose fitting enough so others cannot see the shape of our body.

3. The clothing must not be thin or see-through. It should be thick enough to cover our skin so that it can protect us from the sun or the cold.

4. We cannot cross-dress. This means boys should not wear clothes worn by girls, and girls should not wear clothes worn by boys.

5. Men cannot wear silk or gold jewellery. Women, however, are allowed to wear them.

These are the limits that Allah and His Prophet ﷺ have set for us. We are allowed to wear any clothes as long as they follow these rules. Whatever we wear must be decent and modest. We can wear clothes from any culture. The clothes we choose to wear should be the kind that are worn by the decent and respectable people of that society.

Wearing Islamic clothing does not mean that we have to dress like an Arab or an Indian. Prophet Muhammad ﷺ wore the clothes that were normal for his culture and people. In fact, he even wore non-Arab clothes that did not look strange to the Arabs. For example, he wore a coat with tight sleeves (at-Tirmidhi). This style of coat was worn by the Byzantine people, who were non-Arabs and mainly Christians. The Prophet's open-mindedness shows that he was a universal Prophet who came for people belonging to different races and cultures.

Lesson 27

Intercession

Intercession is when someone helps somebody in need by asking the one in authority to help that person who needs help. On the Day of Judgement, Prophet Muhammad ﷺ will intercede for everyone by asking Allah to start the accountability (Hisab).

The Search for an Intercessor

On the Day of Judgement, when the sun will be close to the gathering place (mahshar), people will be going through a lot of difficulty and hardship. No one will be able to approach Allah because they will fear His anger. So, the people will turn to the Prophets for help. All the people will gather together, and they will put all their hope in the Prophets believing that they will be their intercessors. They will beg them for help, but they will not dare to go to Allah directly.

The people will first go to Prophet Adam عليه السلام and say, "O Prophet Adam! You are the father of humankind. Allah created you with His own hand and He breathed His soul into you. He commanded the angels to prostrate before you. So please intercede for us!" However, Prophet Adam ﷺ will refuse, and he will say, "Verily, my Lord is so angry as though He has never been angry before nor would he be this angry after. Verily, He forbade me to go near that tree, but I made the mistake of going near it. I am concerned with my own self. Go to someone else; go to Nuh."

Then the people will go to Prophet Nuh ﷺ and say, "O Prophet Nuh! You are the first Messenger sent to the earth after Prophet Adam. Allah named you a 'Grateful Servant' so intercede for us with Allah. Do you not see the difficulty we are in?" However, Prophet Nuh ﷺ will refuse, and he will say, "Verily, my Lord is so angry as though He has never been angry before nor would he be this angry after. Verily, I cursed my people with a curse. I am concerned with my own self. Go to someone else; go to Ibrahim."

Then the people will go to Prophet Ibrahim ﵇ and say, "O Prophet Ibrahim! You are the Prophet of Allah and His friend among the people of the earth, so intercede for us with Allah. Do you not see the difficulty we are in?" However, Prophet Ibrahim ﵇ will refuse, and he will say, "Verily, my Lord is so angry as though He has never been angry before nor would he be this angry after. Verily, I had said three things that were not true. I am concerned with my own self. Go to someone else; go to Musa."

Then the people will go to Prophet Musa ﵇ and say, "O Prophet Musa! You are the Messenger of Allah. Allah blessed you with His Message and He spoke to you directly. Intercede for us with Allah. Do you not see the difficulty we are in?" However, Prophet Musa ﵇ will refuse, and he will say, "Verily, my Lord is so angry as though He has never been angry before nor would he be this angry after. Verily, I had accidently killed a person who I had not been ordered to kill. I am concerned with my own self. Go to someone else; go to `Isa." Then the people will go to Prophet `Isa ﵇ and say, "O Prophet `Isa! You are the Messenger of Allah and you spoke to the people in the cradle. You are Allah's Word and you are the Spirit from Him. Intercede for us with Allah. Do you not see the difficulty we are in?" However, Prophet `Isa عليه السلام will refuse, and he will say, "Verily, my Lord is so angry as though He has never been angry before nor would he be this angry after. I am concerned with my own self. Go to someone else; go to Muhammad."

Then the people will go to Prophet Muhammad ﷺ and say, "O Muhammad! You are the Messenger of Allah and the final Prophet. Allah has forgiven you; so, intercede for us with Allah. Do you not see the difficulty we are in?"

Prophet Muhammad ﷺ, however, will not turn away their request. He will say, "I am the one who will intercede."

The Prophet's Intercession

Prophet Muhammad ﷺ will go to the `Arsh (Divine Throne) and fall in prostration before Allah. He will ask for Allah's permission and Allah will give him such glorifications that have not been given to anyone else before him.

Allah will then say, "O Muhammad, raise your head and speak, for you will be listened to. Ask, for you will be granted your request, and intercede, for your intercession will be accepted." The Prophet ﷺ will say, "O Lord! My Ummah! My Ummah!" Allah will then say, "Go and take out of the Hellfire all those people who have faith in their hearts equal to the weight of a barley grain."

After saving those people, Prophet Muhammad ﷺ will return to the `Arsh (Divine Throne) and praise Allah again with the same glorifications while falling in prostration before Him. Allah will say, "O Muhammad, raise your head and speak, for you will be listened to. Ask, for you will be granted your request, and intercede, for your intercession will be accepted." The Prophet ﷺ will say, "O Lord! My Ummah! My Ummah!" Allah will then say, "Go and take out of the Hellfire all those people who have faith in their hearts equal to the weight of a mustard seed."

Prophet Muhammad ﷺ will do this, and then return to Allah again glorifying Him and falling in prostration before Him. Allah will say, "O Muhammad, raise your head and speak, for you will be listened to. Ask, for you will be granted your request, and intercede, for your intercession will be accepted." The Prophet ﷺ will say, "O Lord! My Ummah! My Ummah!" Allah will then say, "Go and take out of the Hellfire all those people who have in their hearts faith equal to even the smallest weight of the mustard seed."

Then the Prophet ﷺ will return a fourth time and ask for the same. And Allah will say, "By my Power and Majesty, I will take out of the Hellfire anyone who has said: 'There is no one worthy of worship except Allah.'" (al-Bukhari and Muslim)

Lesson 28

`Umrah

The fifth pillar of Islam is the Hajj (the Pilgrimage). Pilgrimage is a journey a person goes on to visit a special and holy place. Muslims perform Pilgrimage to Makkah to visit the Ka`bah. The Ka`bah is the House of Allah and anyone who visits it is Allah's guest (Ibn Majah).

The Hajj is performed over five or six days between the 8th and 13th of Dhu al-Hijjah. It is the major pilgrimage. Every Muslim must perform this once in a lifetime if they can afford it. However, Muslims can visit the Ka`bah throughout the rest of the year. They can perform a smaller (minor) pilgrimage known as `Umrah.

The `Umrah: A Step-by-Step Guide

To perform the `Umrah, the first thing you need to do is to come into the state of **Ihram**. The Ihram is a state where some lawful (Halal) things, such as hunting, moving plants or trees, trimming the hair or nails and applying perfume become unlawful (Haram) for you. Without being in a state of Ihram, it is not permissible to perform the `Umrah. You must be in the state of Ihram before entering Makkah.

There is an important border around Makkah called the '**Miqat**'. If you want to perform the `Umrah, you must be in a state of Ihram when you cross this border into Makkah. If a person crosses this border without being in a state of Ihram, he or she will be sinful and will have to pay a penalty, such as sacrificing a sheep or a goat. For pilgrims coming from the West, they should be in a state of Ihram at least 30 minutes before reaching Jeddah by plane.

How to Enter the State of Ihram?

Before entering the state of Ihram, we should prepare ourselves by cleaning our bodies first. It is recommended to have a bath, trim the nails and to wear perfume. This can be done at home before leaving for the airport.

After cleaning the body, the male pilgrim wears two cotton sheets (or any other material), which is either new or washed. One is wrapped around the upper part of the body and the other is wrapped around the lower part of the body. No stitched clothing should be worn; just the two cotton sheets are allowed. The head cannot be covered with a hat. The middle bone of the upper part of the foot and ankle cannot be covered either.

The female pilgrim wears a normal dress. The body must be fully covered except the face, hands and feet. The face is not allowed to be covered in the state of Ihram.

After putting on the Ihram clothing, two units of Nafl prayer are performed. Now you are ready to enter the state of Ihram. The pilgrim enters this state by first making the intention (niyyah) to perform the `Umrah and then by reciting the Talbiyah.

The Talbiyah is a special prayer that is recited by the pilgrim in the state of Ihram. The words of the Talbiyah are:

Labbayk Allaahumma labbayk. Labbayk laa sharika laka labbayk. Innal-hamda wan-ni`mata laka wal-mulk. Laa sharika lak.

لَبَّيْكَ اَللَّهُمَّ لَبَّيْكَ. لَبَّيْكَ لَا شَرِيْكَ لَكَ لَبَّيْكَ.
إِنَّ الْحَمْدَ وَالنِّعْمَةَ لَكَ وَالْمُلْكَ لَا شَرِيْكَ لَكَ

Here I am at Your service, O Lord, here I am. Here I am at Your service and You have no partner. For You alone is all praise and all bounty, and for You alone is the power. You have no partner.

The Talbiyah should be recited three times and continued to be recited until the pilgrim performs the `Umrah. Men recite it loudly and women recite it quietly.

After making the intention and reciting the Talbiyah, the pilgrim enters the state of Ihram. The state of Ihram ends after finishing the `Umrah when the hair is shaved or trimmed.

Performing the Rites of `Umrah

When the pilgrim reaches Makkah he or she goes to the Ka`bah to perform the Tawaf. The Tawaf is an act of worship and it involves going around the Ka`bah seven times in an anticlockwise direction.

Like the Salah, it must be performed in a state of purity (Taharah).

Before starting the Tawaf, the male pilgrim should make sure that the white sheet covering the upper part of the body is worn in a way that the right shoulder is uncovered. This is known as **Idtiba`**.

The starting point for the Tawaf is the Black Stone (al-Hajar al-Aswad) and that is also where it ends.

We start the Tawaf by greeting the Black Stone. We raise our hands in the direction of the Black stone and say 'Bismillaahi wallaahu Akbar'. Now the first circuit of the Tawaf starts.
Men must perform the '**Raml**' in the first three circuits. The Raml is when men walk quickly taking short steps, keeping their chest out and at the same time moving the shoulders like a wrestler.

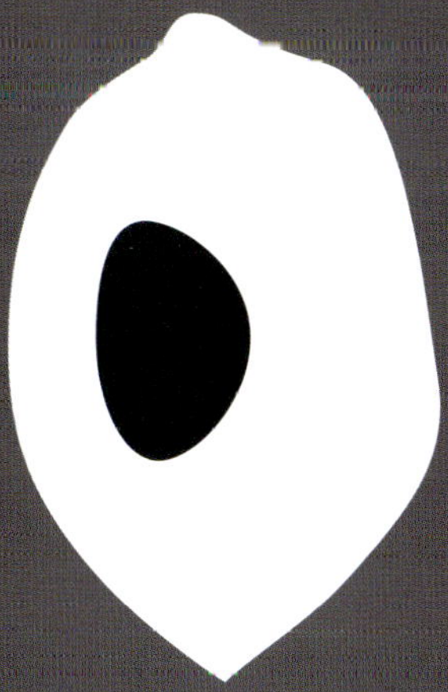

During the Tawaf, you can recite any du`a (supplication) or adkhar (invocation). You should continue making your way round the Ka`bah greeting the Black Stone at the end of each circuit. At the end of the seventh circuit, greet the Black Stone and then find an empty space behind or near the **Maqam Ibrahim**. Perform two units of wajib prayer here to complete the Tawaf.

After completing the Tawaf, drink some **Zamzam** water. Then make your way to Safa to perform the **Sa'i**. You can have a short break if you are tired, but it is best not to without a good reason.

The Sa'i is performed by walking between Safa and Marwah. It is seven circuits, starting from Safa and ending at Marwah. It must be performed between Safa and Marwah and not outside of its borderline; otherwise the Sa'i will not be valid.

Begin the Sa'i by standing at Safa. Face the Qiblah and make the intention to perform the Sa'i. Raise the hands in supplication and pray to Allah. Then make your way towards Marwah. This is the beginning of the first circuit.

Between Safa and Marwah, there are two markers which are shown by green lights. It is recommended to run between them when performing the Sa`i. When you reach Marwah, you have completed the first circuit. Here, you should face the Qiblah and raise your hands in supplication and pray to Allah.

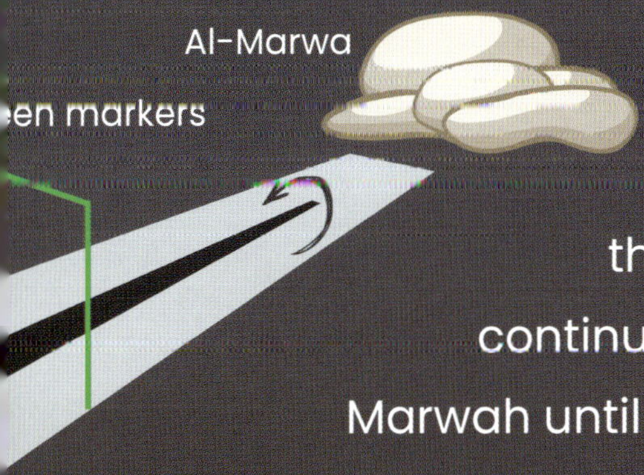

Then make your way towards Safa. This is the beginning of the second circuit. When you reach Safa, the second circuit is over. You continue walking between Safa and Marwah until you complete your seventh circuit at Marwah. Here, at Marwah, the Sa`i is completed, and the `Umrah comes to an end.

After completing the `Umrah, you can come out of the state of Ihram. Men come out of this state by either shaving their head or trimming their hair. Women come out of the state of ihram by cutting their hair only by the length of a fingertip.

When this is done, you are no longer in the state of Ihram, and all the limits of the Ihram are finished.

Lesson 28 / `Umrah

Lesson 29

Sirah: The Battle of Khandaq

For centuries, the Jews were waiting for the arrival of the final Prophet who was mentioned to them in the Torah. Many of them left Syria and Jordan to live in the small town of Yathrib in the middle of Arabia, because they knew from their holy book that the final Prophet would one day emigrate to Yathrib (Madinah).

Over many years, the Jews were at war with their Arab neighbours. They would pray to Allah through the name of the final Prophet asking Allah for victory over their enemies. They used to remind the Arabs that when the final Prophet arrived, they would kill the Arabs. But when the Prophet ﷺ came to them, even after recognising him as the Prophet who was mentioned in the Torah, they disbelieved in him and they rejected his message (al-Baqara 2:89).

The Response of the Jews of Yathrib

Mother of the Believers Safiyyah bint Huyayy mentioned that her father Huyayy bin Akhtab and her uncle Abu Yasir were discussing if Prophet Muhammad ﷺ was the Prophet that was mentioned in the Torah. Her uncle asked her father, "Is it really him?" And her father replied, "By Allah, yes, it is him." "Then what will you do?" her uncle asked. "By Allah, I will be against him as long as I am alive," her father replied.

Many Jews in Yathrib recognised that Prophet Muhammad ﷺ was indeed the Final Prophet predicted to them in the Torah. But they were unable to accept him because the Prophet ﷺ was an Arab and not from their tribe. However, not all the Jews went against the Prophet ﷺ. There were many who also became Muslims.

One of the Jews who became a Muslim was the main rabbi called `Abd Allah bin Salam.

Remembering the moment when the Prophet ﷺ entered Madinah, he said that he praised Allah loudly. His aunty was nearby, and she heard how excited he was. She was cross at him and said, "Woe to you. If you had heard that Prophet Musa arrived, you would not have been any happier." "O aunty, by Allah, he is the brother of Prophet Musa and he is on his religion," `Abd Allah bin Salam replied, "he has been raised with the same religion as him." "O my nephew, is he really the Prophet about whom we were told?" his aunty asked, and he replied, "Yes".

When `Abd Allah bin Salam met the Prophet ﷺ he accepted Islam, but he kept it hidden from the Jews. He then told the Prophet ﷺ of a plan to get the Jews to accept Islam. When the Jews came to meet the Prophet ﷺ, `Abd Allah bin Salam hid in the room. The Prophet ﷺ asked the Jews what the position of `Abd Allah bin Salam was among them, and they replied, "He is our master and the son of our master. He is our rabbi and the most knowledgeable among us."

After they said this, `Abd Allah bin Salam came out of his hiding place and said, "O Jews, fear Allah and accept the message he has brought. By Allah, you know that he is the Prophet whose name and description can be found written in the Torah. I bear witness that he is the Messenger of Allah and I believe in him and accept him." Hearing this, the Jews got angry with `Abd Allah bin Salam and they beat him up. They no longer saw him as their master. After this, `Abd Allah bin Salam made his Islam public to everyone, and his aunty also became a true Muslim like him.

Khaybar Sides With the Quraysh

Even though there was a peace agreement between the Muslim and the Jewish tribes of Madinah, the Jews could not accept the Prophet ﷺ as the leader of the state. The confidence of the Muslims made them uncomfortable.

There was a group of Jews from Khaybar. They belonged to the Banu Nadir. They were banished from Madinah after they had declared war on the Prophet ﷺ. The chiefs of this tribe travelled to Makkah to meet the Quraysh. In this group was the Jewish leader Huyayy bin Akhtab. This group from Khaybar met with the Quraysh and asked them to go to war against the Muslims. They promised to support the Quraysh until the Muslims were forced to leave Madinah.

The Quraysh were happy that the Jews from Khaybar also hated the Muslims and they were happy to work with them to bring an end to Islam. Seeing how friendly they were towards them, the Quraysh asked, "O Jews, you are the people of the book. Tell us, whose religion is better? Ours or Muhammad's?" The Jews replied, "Of course, your religion is better than his, and you have more right to the truth than him." Hearing this from them made the Quraysh even happier and they wasted no time in preparing to attack Madinah.

The Quraysh had an army of four thousand men. The Jews also met with other Arabian tribes, such as the Banu Asad and the Banu Ghatafan in Najd. They persuaded them to also join the battle against the Muslims. Now the total number of soldiers marching towards Madinah was 10,000. Through this battle, the Quraysh hoped to bring an end to Islam once and for all.

The Muslims Prepare for War

The Prophet's uncle al-`Abbas sent a letter to the Prophet ﷺ to warn him about the enormous army on its way to Madinah. The Prophet ﷺ gathered his Companions together to discuss what to do because they had never faced an army as great as this one.

One of the Prophet's Companions was called Salman. He was from Persia. Salman told the Prophet ﷺ that in his land they would dig a trench when they fought against a powerful army. After listening to

Salman, they all agreed to this plan and they started to dig a trench around Madinah.

It was a huge task and they had only six days to complete it. The Muslims worked extremely hard, day and night, to make sure that the trench was finished. During these hard and difficult days, the Companions saw some of the Prophet's miracles, which proved the truthfulness of his prophethood.

Jabir bin `Abd Allah describes that there was a part of the trench in which there was a big rock. The rock was very difficult to move, and the Companions tried their best to move it, but they could not. So, they called the Prophet ﷺ for help. The Prophet ﷺ asked for a pot of water. He then sprinkled water on the rock and prayed to Allah to move the stone. After this, the Companions tried to move the big rock again and they found that it was easy to move!

The Prophet's Miracles

Whilst the trench was being dug, one of the women of Madinah sent her daughter to give dates to her father and uncle who were working at the trench. On the way, she passed by the Prophet ﷺ who asked what she had with her. She replied that she had some dates. The Prophet ﷺ called her and asked her to give the dates to him. She put all the dates in his two blessed hands. There were very few dates that they did not even fill the Prophets blessed hands. The Prophet ﷺ instructed that a cloak be spread out, he put the dates on the cloak and scattered them all over it. Then the Prophet ﷺ called the hundreds of Companions who were digging the trench to eat from it. As the Companions ate, the dates kept on increasing in number until there were so many dates that they were dropping off from the side of the cloak.

On another occasion, one of the Companions asked his wife to cook a sheep because he wanted to invite the Prophet ﷺ for a meal. When she cooked the sheep, the Companion invited the Prophet ﷺ to be his guest. His intention was that only the Prophet ﷺ would eat with him and no one else. However, the Prophet ﷺ invited all his Companions to join them in the meal as well. When the Companion saw this, he became worried because there was only enough meat for a few people. When the meal was ready, the Prophet ﷺ prayed to Allah and started eating. One by one, the Companions took turns in small groups to join in the meal. The meat was only enough for a few people, but hundreds of Companions ate till they were full.

In one part of the trench, the Prophet ﷺ took a pick-axe and hit a large stone. There was a flash of light. Then the Prophet ﷺ hit it again, and there was another flash of light. This happened again for a third time. Salman, the Companion from Persia, asked the Prophet ﷺ about the three flashes of light. The Prophet ﷺ replied, "In the first flash, Allah promised me the conquest of Yemen; in the second flash, He promised me the conquest of Syria and the West, and in the third flash, He promised me the conquest of the East."

When the hypocrites heard this, they made fun out of the Muslims. They questioned how the Muslims could believe that they will conquer and take over the great empires of Rome and Persia, when here they were fighting for their survival. But the Muslims had solid belief and trust in Allah. Even in this difficult time, when it looked like their world was coming to an end, they knew that the light of Islam would continue to shine brightly for the future. Several years after the Prophet ﷺ passed away, Allah fulfilled this promise and the Muslims became masters of a huge empire that spread as far as Spain in the west and India in the east.

New Style of Warfare

When the Arab tribes reached Madinah and saw the huge trench, they were surprised by what they saw. They did not know how to respond to this new way of war that the Muslims were following. They tried to cross over the trench with their horses, but they were unable to because the horses barely reached the other side. Anyone who dared to approach the trench was met with a shower of arrows. The enemy army had reached a deadlock. They did not know what to do except to wait on the other side of the trench, but they could not stay for long because they were not prepared for a battle like this one.

The Quraysh depended on the Jews for help. Huyayy bin Akhtab persuaded the Jewish tribe of Banu Qurayzah to break their peace agreement with the Muslims and to attack Madinah from inside. At first, the leader of Banu Qurayzah, Ka`b bin Asad refused to meet Huyayy, because he did not want to break the union with the Muslims. Eventually

Ka`b agreed and he announced publicly that the peace treaty between them and the Muslims was broken. When the news of Banu Qurayzah's disloyalty reached the Prophet ﷺ, he was deeply saddened by it.

The Quraysh continued to wait on the other side of the trench. Days passed by and they were running out of supplies. Their horses and camels were dying. On the 27th night, there was a strong wind and it was extremely cold. No fire could be seen in any of the tents and everyone was huddling together for heat. The strong wind made the horses and camels panic and some of them caused chaos in the camps stamping on the enemy soldiers. Abu Sufyan announced he was returning to Makkah because he could not see any end to the situation. They could not bear it anymore. Before the sun had risen the next day, they had packed up their camps and quickly made their way back home.

In the morning, when the sun rose, the Muslims

saw the battlefield abandoned by the enemy. They praised Allah for protecting them from their enemies and they returned home. As the Prophet ﷺ was returning to his house, he saw Angel Jibra'il who said, "The angels have not yet put down their swords. Allah commands that you go to the Banu Qurayzah." So, the Prophet ﷺ and his Companions went to the Banu Qurayzah who were hiding inside, and they surrounded their fortress.

The Siege of Banu Qurayzah

The siege lasted for 25 nights. The Banu Qurayzah knew that they had to give themselves up to the

Muslims because they could not stay inside for much longer. Their leader, Ka`b bin Asad, asked his tribe what they wanted to do. He gave them three options: the first option was to accept Islam and become Muslims; the second option was to kill their own women and children and to go outside and fight against the Muslims; and the third option was to give themselves up to the Prophet ﷺ and to let him decide what punishment to give them.

The Banu Qurayzah rejected the first two options. They chose the third option which was to give themselves up and to let the Prophet ﷺ decide what to do with them.

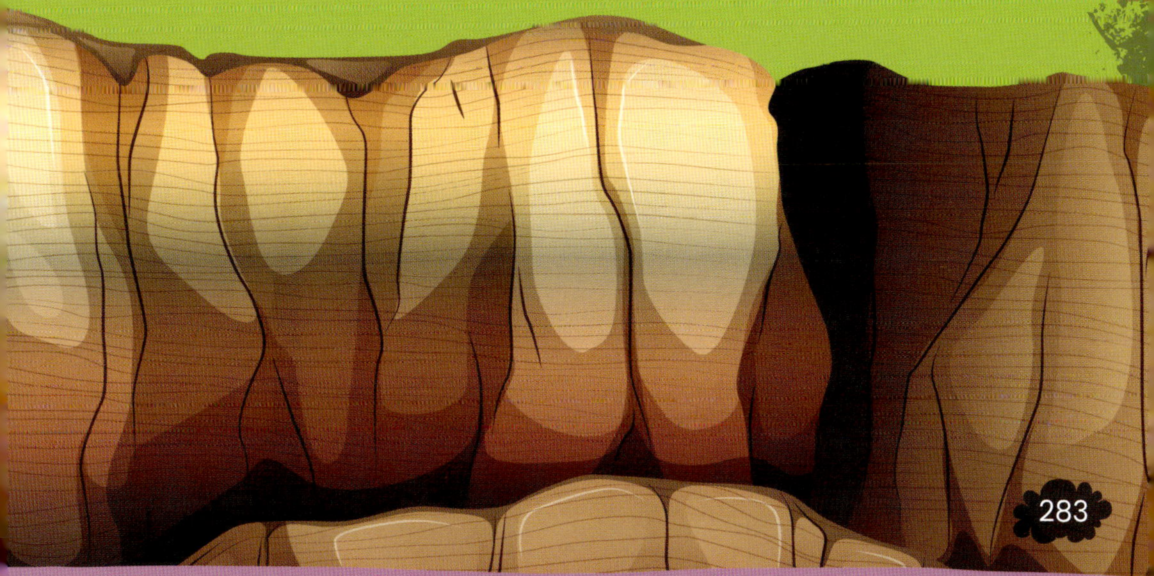

There were many young people from the Banu Qurayzah who were encouraged by their rabbis who told them about the coming of the Prophet ﷺ. These young people chose to become Muslims and follow the Prophet ﷺ instead of following their tribe.

When the Banu Qurayzah gave themselves up, the Prophet ﷺ chose Sa`d bin Mu`adh to be a judge over them. Sa`d used to be friends with the Banu Qurayzah before he became a Muslim, so he knew them very well. He ruled that the men be sentenced to death for their crimes and the women and children should be taken as prisoners of war.

He decided this because he saw how many of the ransomed prisoners from previous wars returned later in the battle of Uhud and Khandaq to fight against the

Muslims. So, Sa`d gave this ruling because he did not want them to plan with the Quraysh to attack the Muslims again in the future.

Lesson 30

Halal and Haram (Part Two)

Allah has created many things for us to eat and drink, such as fruits, vegetables and the meat of animals. He has made all this for us to enjoy. We should be thankful to Him for the blessing of food.

In the Qur'an, Allah tells us to eat from the food that is lawful (halal) and pure (tayyib) (al-Baqara 2:168). There are some types of food and drink that are haram (unlawful) in Islam.

The following types of food and drink are **haram** (**unlawful**):

1. Pork/bacon/ham
2. Animals and birds that eat meat

3. Flowing blood
4. Dead animals

5. Animals that are not slaughtered in the name of Allah

6. Alcoholic Drinks

Apart from the things listed above, everything else is halal for us to eat and drink. There are many more things that are lawful (halal) for us to eat than the things that are unlawful (haram).

When we go to supermarkets or shops, we should check the ingredients of the food that we buy. None of the food that you buy should contain anything haram (unlawful). One of the best ways to know if the food that we eat is halal is to see if there is a **halal** or **vegetarian** sign on the

packaging. However, we must still be careful when there is a vegetarian sign as sometimes the food can have wine in it. So, we should always check the ingredients before buying.

Halal Meat

As Muslims, we must be careful about the type of meat that we eat. We only eat meat that is good for our body and soul. Whatever we eat has an effect on our behaviour and this is why we eat some meat and not others.

For example, the meat of animals and birds that eat other animals is unlawful, because these animals are violent and fierce and we do not want these characteristics in ourselves. Pig meat is unlawful because pigs are greedy and unclean, they do not care about what they eat or do, and we do not want to have these characteristics.

The animals that are lawful for us are the type that eat grass and leaves and do not hurt others with their teeth. They have good characteristics which we want. This is why we eat their meat and drink their milk and not the meat or milk of the other animals.

The Ritual Slaughter

When we want to eat the meat of halal animals, we have to slaughter the animal and recite the name of Allah first. Doing this is called '**dhabiha**' in Arabic. By doing the dhabiha the animal becomes halal for us to eat. If an animal is slaughtered incorrectly or if it is slaughtered in the name of a false god or an idol, it would become haram for us to eat.

The animals that Muslims eat must be slaughtered in a special way. The animal must be alive at the time of slaughter, because dead animals are unlawful (haram) to eat.

The purpose of the slaughter is to remove the blood because flowing blood is not pure. We remove the blood by sacrificing the animal and this makes its meat pure and clean.

Islam does not permit us to harm animals. While it is alive we must be kind to it and not treat it badly. The way we treat the animal is important because by treating it well, the animal's meat will be blessed for our body and soul.

When we slaughter the animal, we give it water to drink and calm it down first. We do not slaughter it in front of other animals or show it the knife that we are going to use.

The Qur'an has allowed Muslims to eat the meat that is slaughtered by the **Ahl al-Kitab (the People of the Book)** which are the Jews and the Christians. The Jews have similar laws to Muslims and they also slaughter their meat and recite God's name. They call their meat 'kosher', which means 'fit'. This is the Jewish version of halal, and Muslims are allowed to eat it as well.

Though the meat of the Ahl al-Kitab (the People of the Book) is lawful, we must take extra precaution before eating it. Many of the Ahl al-Kitab today do not follow the rules of animal slaughter (dhabiha). So, we should only eat the meat slaughtered by them if we are certain that the animal has been slaughtered properly.

Eating Fish

Prophet Muhammad ﷺ allowed us to eat fish. It is not possible to do the dhabiha (ritual slaughter) on fishes. When they are taken out of the water, they die straightaway. Even though fish cannot be slaughtered like the other halal animals, Prophet Muhammad ﷺ allowed his Ummah to eat fish and he made it halal (lawful) for Muslims.

Fish is lawful to eat because Prophet Muhammad ﷺ made it lawful; without the Sunnah of the

Prophet ﷺ fish would not have been halal. This shows us the importance of the Sunnah in Islam. If someone says it is not important to follow the Sunnah of the Prophet ﷺ and that we should follow only the Qur'an, then that person should not eat fish, because fish was made halal by the Sunnah and not by the Qur'an.

Alcoholic Drinks

Muslims are not allowed to drink alcohol. Alcoholic drinks make people lose control of their senses. When a person is drunk they do not realise what they are doing or saying. They might go home to their family and hurt them or make them sad and upset through their uncontrollable behaviour. Allah made alcoholic drinks unlawful (haram) for us because He wants us to be in control of our senses so that we always know what we are saying and doing.

Eating Pure Foods

In the Qur'an, Allah tells us not to eat only the food that is **lawful (halal)**, but to also eat food that is **pure (tayyib)**. Prophet Muhammad ﷺ explained the meaning of this through his Sunnah. He taught us that our body has a right over us and it is a trust from Allah. We must look after our body by eating good and healthy food that nourishes it and keeps us healthy. Prophet Muhammad ﷺ used to eat more plant-based food and less meat.

Here are some important guidelines that we should try to follow:

- Try not to eat junk food.
- Try to eat more home cooked food.
- Choose fresh food instead of processed food which has chemicals in it.
- Eat more vegetables and less meat.